Editorial Foreword

Death, and awareness of death; these are two attributes of the human condition with which every society must come to terms. They have been dealt with in as many different ways as there have been separate cultures, and even within cultures the beliefs and customs which are employed to domesticate these unnerving realities can be seen to change from one historical period to the next.

If one regards myth and ritual as the resort to fantasy and to magical acts in order to allay the anxieties provoked by events which man cannot understand or control, then it is not surprising that in every society death is associated with beliefs and observances of very great emotional significance.

Anthropologists have shown us how societies, both primitive and advanced, single out successive stages of man's life as having particular importance, and how they mark the moment of entry into each such stage with institutionalized ceremonials, known as *rites de passage*. The change of status may involve an irreversible biological event, as at birth, puberty and death; or it may be socially defined, as at marriage, inheritance or election to office: but all such changes of status, with one exception, imply that the individual enters into a new mode of relationship with his fellow-men. The exception, of course, is death. Here the human actor seems to have relinquished his role, but he is seldom allowed to do so immediately. His life's story is not allowed to come to an abrupt conclusion, but must be rounded off with appropriate after-death ceremonial.

The beliefs and practices surrounding death can be seen to serve two purposes. Firstly, they assuage its frightening aspects by fitting it in to a coherent system of values, usually linked with the concept of life after death. Secondly, they rally the support of the extended family or kin to comfort and support those who have been bereaved.

Not unnaturally, funerary ceremonial plays an especially important part in the life of primitive societies, where death is no less frightening because it is of relatively frequent occurrence. Many observers have remarked the rapid decline in our own society, during the present century, of attention paid to the ceremonial aspect of death. This change has come at a time when the average expectation of life has been dramatically increased. Now, as never before, many people in our society can reach adulthood without having had close personal acquaintance with death. At the same time, we have also seen a sharp decline in the authority of traditional religious beliefs, one of whose important functions was to allay the pain and fear of death. For most people, the decay of religious belief has not prompted any alternative philosophy: instead of trying to answer the ultimate questions, they have simply tended to postpone or ignore them. As a result, when death does come, it tends to catch us more than ever unprepared. Recent research has shown that bereavement, if not adequately coped with, can seriously affect the mental and physical health of the survivors.

During the past fifty years, the incidence of mortality has been radically altered but it now appears to be settling down to a new rhythm. In previous generations, death was a not uncommon hazard of childhood, of child-bearing and of adults in the prime of life: to some extent, this is still true – coronary thrombosis, for example, kills many fathers of young families – but many more people live to old age before encountering their mortal illness. It is particularly their problems, and those of the families who have to take care of their older members, with which this book is concerned.

Among all the ways of dealing with death, the one most surely doomed to failure is the attempt to ignore it. Professor Hinton,

who has had even more intimate acquaintance with dying patients
than have most doctors, here sets out to give a balanced, truthful
picture of how people approach death in our post-war society.
Part of the picture is ugly, and part of it is painful. He is able to
show that doctors, nurses and relatives can do a great deal to
mitigate the physical and mental suffering which accompanies so
many terminal illnesses – but that in order to do so, they must have
the fortitude to recognize such suffering and not simply to cover it
up or persuade themselves that it does not exist.

This book, therefore, not only gives us the medical and social
facts about death and dying in our society in the middle of the
twentieth century, but also contains a great deal of information
which can be of immediate, practical use to those who have to face
this problem in their personal or family life.

G. M. CARSTAIRS

1 Introduction

Although we may accept the idea of death in the abstract without disquiet, sooner or later each of us will be obliged to face the disturbing personal issues that arise. Some of these are introduced through the words and experiences of two people who died not long ago.

The first person died quite peacefully. She was a retired teacher, who throughout her life had been concerned to help others as much as she could. While dying of cancer, although her physical condition began to deteriorate rapidly, she was quite alert and welcomed visitors to her bedside. Like most people, when she was given the opportunity to talk freely about her illness and her feelings she was glad to do so. 'I know I've got cancer; it's spreading over my body. I want to see Mr — [her consultant surgeon] because I don't want just to be kept alive with radium. I know I'm going to go; I accept it, I'm not miserable about it.'

This message was passed on to her surgeon, a doctor strongly concerned with his patients' general welfare as well as with the treatment of their diseases. As far as the physical treatment was concerned, he willingly agreed with his patient's viewpoint that there was little he could do to prolong any worth-while life. He added that the pressure of work prevented him from visiting her again to talk further about it. This was reasonable enough from the practical point of view, but he also indicated that he was not sorry to have grounds to avoid such an interview. His patient had considerable understanding of how he might feel. 'I know you doctors can't say. It's your job to save lives.'

She herself did not always want to admit that she was dying. In subsequent conversations, in spite of her earlier awareness of the true nature of her illness, she would often speak in a light wondering fashion about her symptoms as if she could not begin to guess what caused them. There were times when she wanted to maintain this pretence with others and not refer to her real state. What little pain she had was kept under control quite easily and she wanted to return home, where she died within a few days.

The circumstances of the other patient were, unfortunately, very different. He had only recently retired, and was in hospital, dying in considerable distress. He had delayed seeking medical advice for his heart failure because his views, derived from Christian Science, had led him to believe it possible to overcome by faith any threat to his health or life. It suddenly became apparent to him, in his exhausted, breathless state, that, regardless of the conviction that he wanted to uphold, he was still getting worse and might well be dying. He saw a doctor and was hastily admitted to hospital. He was very frightened and troubled and said, 'I thought something was going to happen last night – I don't want to pass on yet.' A friend described how this man's faith had left him, and indeed it was clear how spiritually lost and guilty he felt. He did die within a few days, and until consciousness began to ebb, he suffered a good deal. He only obtained partial relief from the oppressive exhaustion brought on by his incurable illness. Nor did he regain comfort in the faith that had failed him and that he had failed.

The experiences of these two people reveal some of the problems associated with dying, including those that hinge on avoiding thoughts of death. Clearly this evasion has its benefits, otherwise it would not be so widespread. As it can be distressing for the dying to contemplate their death they often act as if they will recover. Although the courageous woman with cancer had openly acknowledged that she was dying, she also resorted to a little make-believe on some occasions – there was no need for her to diminish her remaining life by perversely brooding over death.

The man had gained comfort during his lifetime by denying that death was inevitable. In this he had been more extreme than is usual. Most people freely admit that all men will die, but they are reluctant to consider too closely their own death or the death of those they love, except as events in a rather distant future. People want to stay alive and they take the obvious practical measures to preserve life. Not content with their own efforts, which cannot prevent death for ever, many pray for some divine intervention to shield them. But religions may promise even more: they allow people to believe that they can for ever avoid total death. Many faiths assert that man does not wholly die and they help the faithful by preparing them for the end of their mortal existence.

Attempts to deny death and mortality are not wholly successful, however, and when they fail they can bring increased distress. The man who had tried so hard during his life to use a religion to deny that he could die, rather than accept that his life on earth would end, was ill-prepared for death when it came. He suffered because of this. Very many people in our culture are not prepared to meet their death, although they may triumphantly endure their last days by sheer courage; and in some respects, modern circumstances do assist us to avoid the disturbing thought of our own death – with longer lives and better health, immediate contact with death and dying is likely to come less frequently. Nevertheless there are other features of our culture which do not allow us to forget death. Tragedies involving loss of life are announced every day in newspapers, pictures of dead bodies appear with increasing frequency in magazines and on television, there is talk of weapons that will destroy millions of lives and so on. The majority of people can still regard such events as unlikely to impinge directly on their own lives. The personal significance of death is still warded off; the descriptions of tragic deaths are heard with distant interest, murder stories are read for pleasure and serious thoughts about personal death do not often get far beyond making financial provision 'just in case'.

Reluctance to face death brings one undeniable evil. When people are disinclined to get involved in the personal problems of the dying, mortally ill people suffer more. In one way it was endured by the dying woman, who for a long time could not find anyone willing to talk about the important things concerning her approaching death. Her experience occurs commonly enough, but it was not as bad as that of many mortally ill who see people with-drawing from them almost as if they were already partly dead. If those who care for a dying patient feel too much unease in his presence, they cannot tend him as completely as they should. They may be haunted by the fear that their patient will ask about his illness or speak of dying, and they have no idea what to say to him. Some doctors are reluctant to stay long near the dying because they only like to talk to patients in terms of cure. They are apt to see death as a medical failure, and retreat too hastily.

Another great problem of the dying, revealed in the brief account of those two people, is the physical suffering that may occur in the terminal illness. The woman with cancer was fortun-ate. The pain and the discomfort that sometimes arose from the localized swellings due to her disease were adequately relieved by treatments familiar to all doctors. Her stable personality helped her to cope with the nearness of death without any great emotional distress. She was able to share some of her feelings with those who felt sympathy. The man was less fortunate. Although he did not have to endure it for long, his physical discomfort was bad at times, and he had a mental anguish that was hard to allay.

Considerable knowledge and skill is available to relieve distress caused by disease. To bring comfort, sometimes without curing, is a very important part of the work of nurses and doctors. A few, owing to their particular aptitude, experience or vocation, gain a special skill. Nevertheless, since some people still suffer in their last illness, clearly we either do not know enough or we fail to give the help that is within our power. Prejudice hinders. In the case of the dying it is only too easy to apply preconceived ideas without considering any alternative. One or two emotion-laden experiences with the dying can produce convictions about the proper manage-ment of patients that no amount of subsequent information will alter. Such established attitudes even lead to denying the need for more knowledge.

As a first step to improving our care we need to know the nature and degree of distress that does occur in fatal illness. Search for this sort of information soon shows that well-established know-ledge is scanty; it is a disturbing ignorance. Only in the last few years have people been prepared to investigate this problem in any systematic fashion. The impersonal aspects of the data have often been available for some time. For instance, it is not too difficult to find out how long on average a patient survives with any particular fatal disorder. This type of information about the progress of diseases is insufficient, and, more recently, some attention has been focused on the experiences of the ill people concerned.

There has been a broad survey of the terminal care available in hospitals and homes in Britain, and this report does not foster complacency.[87] The distress of patients dying of cancer has been assessed in other surveys in the United States[89] and in Britain.[94] These reports have indicated that although some die quite peacefully, much more help is required. The inquiry by the Marie Curie Foundation and the Queen's Institute of District Nursing[94] is particularly disquieting: it shows clearly that many people suffer more than they should during their terminal illness at home. There have been one or two other reports of the home care of the dying either by general practitioners[211] or by hospital staff who have kept in touch with their patients after they have left their immediate care. [11, 169] The Institute for Social Studies in Medical Care has just completed a survey of the terminal care received by a sample of people dying in Britain.[36] Again it is a picture of only partial success.

Hospital care is far from perfect. Observations of a number of elderly patients dying in a geriatric unit revealed that quite a number were in considerable discomfort.[51] A study carried out with patients dying in a teaching hospital confirmed that although they were helped a good deal, there is little reason to be satisfied with our present achievements.[80] One doctor, writing of her experiences in a well-run hospital for the dying, has shown that it is possible to care successfully for dying patients, given the will and adequate training.[173] There is reason to believe that in many institutions the dying get a great deal less solicitude.

These few available studies, and one or two others that will be discussed in this book, confirm that a significant proportion of people die in discomfort. This immediately provokes a series of questions. What are the causes of their suffering? Do we fail to provide adequate care for the dying? What is done to help those in unusual anguish? What treatments are believed to bring most relief; are they favoured because they happen to be in vogue, or because there is unequivocal evidence of their supremacy? How early should pain-relieving drugs be started, how frequently given, and should they be increased liberally? Are dying people in general better cared for at home or in hospital? Which people should be admitted to hospital, and what sort of hospital, what sort of ward? Are there enough people and facilities to look after those who are dying?

To begin to answer these and other questions concerning physical suffering is hard enough, but the problem of relieving any emotional distress is even more complex. Some of the reports mentioned include references to the patients' psychological state. Since this book was first published, two further books have focused attention on assessing the psychological[106] or social[22] aspects of dying. These and other publications, including two American journals specializing in matters of death and dying, indicate a continued growth of concern over the care of the dying.

From the available reports the general impression is that although many die at peace with themselves, as did the woman mentioned early in this chapter, mental anguish, such as the dying man experienced, is not rare. So again the questions spill out. What allows one person to relinquish life easily while another does not want to let go? Are they mainly troubled by fear or sadness? What do they fear, is it a dread of physical suffering or is it a fear of death? Are they troubled because of their uncertainty, or is it that they feel there is a conspiracy to keep the truth from them? Can we relieve their sorrow? Should we tell them that they are dying? Do they already know? If they suspect that they will not recover, should the outcome of the illness be discussed openly with them? How should the matter be raised, by whom, with whom, how often?

While only few attempts are made to define and solve these issues, they will still arouse the fear and prejudice due to ignorance. The shortage of adequate knowledge is understandable. To begin with, it is so difficult to measure suffering, to know if other people's pains have changed a little, or to know if their nausea has been made a bit more bearable or hardly altered at all. Physical symptoms are very difficult to quantify, but the assessment of the emotional state of a dying person is even more unsatisfactory – our methods resemble those attempts to describe a painting by particularizing one or two features to sum up the whole picture in a few fashionable words. Our present state of psychological knowledge allows us to measure one or two aspects of the mental state, but any comprehensive account of a person's psychological state is unattainable. Relevant features such as fear, courage, depression or acceptance of dying can only be assessed in a very crude fashion.

Many would-be investigators are deterred more by their unwillingness to study people who are dying than by the lack of precise measurements.[83] As well as the innate desire to avoid having much to do with death, there is a reluctance to appear intrusive with careful systematic studies in an intensely personal situation. No one wants to inflict embarrassment and emotional pain on dying patients, and so people are chary of embarking on frank discussion to learn what the dying feel or suspect. Also, there is the saddening prospect of visiting, and getting to know and like, a number of people who are going to die soon. Nevertheless, we do need to know more in order to help the dying.

This book is an attempt to gather together some of the available knowledge and ideas on death. It has not been an easy task because, among other reasons, the subject merges with so many fields of human behaviour. The main emphasis has been upon aspects relevant to dying – to the one who is dying, to those about him and to those who will mourn his death. It seemed as well to start with a brief account of some human feelings and ideas about death, hence Chapters 2, 3 and 4. Whatever happens to the dying, or those near by, their previous attitudes to death will colour this experience.

The second part of the book is concerned with the way that people die. Besides a short discussion of the causes of death, it describes the manner in which people face their own death, and the suffering that some of the fatally ill experience. The third part,

Chapters 9 to 12, is about the care of the dying and is, of course, closely linked with the preceding part. People can spend their last days in comfort and peace of mind, or they can suffer. We need to help those who face considerable physical or mental distress. The present achievements, failures and problems of care are surveyed.

The last part of the book considers the people who are left behind when someone dear to them has died, with the many more reactions to bereavement than simple grief and the different ways of taking up the altered pattern of living.

Attitudes to Death

2 Fear of Death and Dying

The emotions aroused by death are legion – fear, sorrow, anger, despair, resentment, resignation, defiance, pity, avarice, triumph, helplessness and, to some degree, practically any emotion that there is. The commonest one is fear. Sorrow is another important theme, felt when something worthwhile is lost, when a precious life is finished. Anger also keeps close company with death, both the anger than can culminate in killing and the resentment at death which takes away pleasure and promise. In this book sorrow and anger will be further discussed in later chapters, in relation to the feelings of the dying and the bereaved.

FEAR AND EVASION OF DEATH

Much of the anxiety that the prospect of death arouses is normal and has a biological value. Were this fear absent, life would be risked unnecessarily and premature death would come too often for racial survival. It seems to be a part of the human constitution and necessary for individual existence. It originates in part from genetically determined instincts, and in part from experience. One of the most important influences in the developing fear of death will be the child's relationship to the parents. The child is influenced not only by parental example and training, but also by the degree of emotional security felt.

In children, an apprehension of death becomes apparent from about the age of five. In these early years their conception of death is, of course, ill-formulated, but they may develop fears of going to sleep and not waking up, of being killed by burglars, of drowning, and of ghosts from the dead. Such fears may be precipitated by a death in the household or by attendance at a funeral, but often there is no obvious cause.[34] Children between the ages of five and nine years often conceive death as a person or some pale, perhaps frightening figure.[138]

On the whole children are not unduly evasive of the thought of death and they are usually quite prepared to speak of it. In a psychologist's study of children's views on death many were found to mention the matter quite spontaneously.[8] The parents recorded any relevant conversations and showed that their children frequently referred to death – the comments often came at bath time. In a more formal part of this particular investigation when the word 'dead' was added to the list of words in a vocabulary test, this word seemed to be accepted quite readily; only 2 out of 91 children appeared to avoid it deliberately.

It is obvious in everyday life, of course, that adults often avoid the mention of death when it has a personal connotation. It is very rare to talk of another's death in his presence. Freud commented that this tendency was more marked if the death would bring about personal gain.[56] When speaking of those we love, we resort to euphemisms that avoid the finality of dying: 'pass on', 'depart this life', 'go to heaven', and so on. If someone speaks of his own death, he is kindly but hastily reassured that this will not be yet awhile. This dissimulation may bring a temporary but not wholly successful ease from the painful subject. The hidden anxiety over death may arise in a disguised form without the original source of fear being recognized. Moreover, the continued evasion of thoughts of death may contribute to a greater distress when death confronts in a way that cannot be denied.[56]

Young adults have less reason to think much of death. Why should they, when they have so much life ahead? While they are discovering and using their increasing abilities, thoughts of death seem irrelevant. This impression is confirmed by the various studies of people's attitudes to death. For instance, in one investigation of students more than 90 per cent said that they rarely thought about death in a personal way,[133] whereas in two studies of the elderly only 30 or 40 per cent kept it from their thoughts.[53, 193] The greater tendency of older people to consider death was shown again in a recent study from Chicago where a sample of over a thousand people were interviewed.[164] These people reported that their thoughts ordinarily were more likely to be of matters of finance, the world situation and so on, rather than questions related to death, but they were very prepared to discuss death at some length. Commonly, death was regarded more as a prolonged sleep than a source of suffering and the main burden fell on the survivors. Most people thought plans should be made in preparation for death, 70 per cent had life insurance, a quarter had made a will, a quarter already had some funeral or cemetery arrangements and a half had spoken about death to their nearest relatives. These trends were more apparent in the older people and in the better educated.

The author of this recent report gained the impression that people were discussing death more openly and the taboo on the topic of death was being relaxed. It does contrast to some extent with a Mass-Observation study carried out in Britain some years ago.[145] In this earlier investigation, several of the people, asked their views on death and dying, said that they could not consider the topic, giving such replies as, 'I – switch my thoughts in other directions', 'I try to think as little as possible about death and dying'. A minority of this group, preoccupied with death though not necessarily in a troubled spirit, kept returning to this unsolved riddle.

Many people say that it is not so much death as dying that they fear and those who associate it with ideas of violence often find death too fearful to even contemplate.[54] If dying is thought of as suffering, then it undoubtedly arouses fear; when people have been asked how they wish to die, the almost universal hope has been for a swift, peaceful exit from life. For instance, 90 per cent of one group of people said that they wished to die quickly and so avoid suffering. The common desire was to pass away peacefully during sleep, although some wished for a time for farewells.[53]

In fact fatal conditions are often remarkably free from discomfort. There are the often quoted words of the dying William

Hunter, physician and anatomist, 'If I had strength enough to hold a pen, I would write how easy and pleasant a thing it is to die.' Ryle has written in his essay *Fears May Be Liars* that distress is often unreasonably attributed to the dying by the spectators, who are naturally anxious and dreading the coming bereavement.[170] Friends and relatives of the dying usually have little knowledge of the protective function of diminished consciousness. Someone about to die may look so ill, or be so confused in mind, that the onlookers mistake this for suffering, and feel helpless because of their inability to relieve an imagined distress.

The image of dying reflected in such a phrase as 'death agony', with its spectacular but distorted picture, is far too extreme, built up in part by the significance of the occasion rather than the reality of the situation, and often deliberately embellished for the sake of drama. Nevertheless, many do suffer a lot in their mortal illness. It justifies some anxiety, and those who have known or witnessed a distressful end to life cannot be sure that their own dying will not be equally painful or worse.

FEAR OF THE DEAD

Another sort of fear, apparent among the complex misgivings over death, concerns dead bodies and spirits. This is less straight-forward than the fear of dying. The dead inspire a host of intense but mixed emotions. As with other matters fundamental to life's pattern, such as sexual activity, there is the apparently paradoxical association of feelings like reverence and disgust, inspiration and fear. This mixture of feelings is not only experienced by the individual but also reflected in the social structure, in its taboos and religious practices. We may perhaps better understand these complex and ambivalent emotions by first considering the ideas of children and primitive peoples.

Children's responses to the dead reveal the early beginnings of these conflicting feelings. Often they show an almost macabre matter-of-fact attitude coupled with intense internal fears. A re-trospective examination of childhood feelings about death was conducted by Caprio, who had been interested in the ethnological

aspects of this subject.[33, 34] Many of the children had experienced
terror at the time of a funeral, especially when they had seen or
touched the corpse, or even kissed the body good-bye – observances more common in the United States, where this study was
made, than in Britain. The change from the living person they
knew to a dead body could be bewildering and shocking. After
their contact with death, there was often a fear of darkness with
the archetypal fear that sleep might turn to death. Caprio was so
impressed by this evidence of childhood terror that he advised
against pressing children to attend funerals or to kiss the departed
one, and warned that threats of hell should not be voiced to
children.

In some primitive cultures the attitudes to the dead body, the
post-mortem changes and the spiritual existence of the deceased
are well defined. Fear is not an inevitable accompaniment to
death, although it lurks near by. It has been found in many ethno-
graphic areas – and clearly described among the Indonesian peoples
by the social anthropologist Hertz – that death is not regarded as
an instant change from mortal life to spiritual eternity.[78] Although
the spirit leaves the body at the time of death, all is not over; the
spirit has not reached its destination. It will not do this until the
dead body has reached a certain state, usually that of clean dry
bones. Until this time the body must be properly cared for by the
appropriate mourners. The soul remains on earth in the vicinity of
the body, retaining certain rights in the community and requiring
particular observances from the mourners. At the end of this
transitional period a final funeral ceremony will mark the departure of the soul of the deceased to its appointed place. It may
then become a benevolent or, perhaps, an inscrutable influence
among ancestral spirits.

During the process there are several potential sources of fear.
The dead body is treated by the tribe as both an object of solicitude
and a source of anxiety. It is particularly vulnerable to the attack of
evil spirits and needs to be defended and a constant watch maintained. After cleansing the body and closing the eyes and the
bodily orifices a number of other hygienic rituals must be performed until decomposition is complete. At the same time, the

corpse has its own potential evil power, perhaps linked with
the noxious smell, and this may escape to strike the living. The
mourners themselves are believed by the community to carry some
of this fearful contagion and may have to live apart and observe
various taboos.

While awaiting the final ceremony which will end its restlessness, the soul of the dead person is unquiet and apt to become
malicious. The spirit may remember past wrongs and may watch to
ensure that relatives fulfil their duties. The spirit still participates
in an earthly existence: food must be put out for him and the widow
remains his wife. Neglect will be met by vengeance from the
wandering soul. The final ceremonies, which show the community's respect for the dead and conclude the period of mourning, are therefore also attended by a feeling of relief from anxiety.
The rites facilitate the spirit's journey to its proper rest-
ing place, assuring the departing soul of the goodwill of
the living and preventing the ghost from bringing mischief upon
them.

Although the departed spirit of a previous member of a tribe is
usually considered to be benevolent, occasionally it is thought to
be malevolent. The reasons given for fearing certain ghosts are
common to many primitive – and not so primitive – communities
throughout the world. Some spirits are believed to remain spiteful
and terrible for ever, because of the dead person's original nature
or the way in which he died. For instance, in some West African
tribes, the ghosts of those who have died violently, perhaps
drowned or killed by their own hand, are potent sources of fear.
Likewise people who have been notoriously bad during their lives
may well become spirits who work evil.[130] If the required rites for
the dead are neglected, the soul may become vindictive. There are
ways of counteracting the threats from the dead. In one East
African tribe, for example, the shaman or witch doctor may be
able to recognize the restless spirit which has been responsible for
bringing illness, shame or death to the tribe. He may find that a
grave has been neglected, thus angering the dead person's spirit,
which is normally located in a small shrine at the head of the grave
until it is reborn as a child two years later. The shaman will, by

various rituals, propitiate the ghost, or even capture it to eliminate the fearful scourge.[13]

It is easy enough for us to view with condescension some of the primitive tribesman's fears of the dead. Nevertheless few civilized people are wholly free of some vague apprehensions of the dead, even if they deny having such irrational timorous thoughts. In our culture, the dead do not often arouse the emotion of naked fear, but corpses, cemeteries or the possibility of ghosts are usually regarded with some aversion.

We have other misgivings, sometimes fear or horror, over the altered state of the body when someone dies. If the body has been disfigured by disease or injury, people may shrink with dismay from the awful change. The idea of a post-mortem examination on someone who was loved can be very troubling. This fear can merge with the concern over future spiritual existence. It is not uncommon for people to imagine or firmly believe that the dead will be resurrected in their human form. To be disfigured threatens the promise of eternal life. There has even been terror that death in war from explosives will destroy not only the body but the promise of eternity. If a dead body is still treated as though it were a person held in high regard, the changes in that body will be viewed with deep concern.

OTHER FEARS DISPLACED ON TO DEATH

Most people will experience from time to time normal fears about death, either when some symptom or particular situation holds a fatal threat or when it seems that a valued person may die. Sometimes an individual's fear of death seems quite abnormal – though there is no easy distinction between normal and abnormal fears of death.[2][19] The magnified fear of death has usually gathered its unreasonable strength from another source of anxiety.

It is easy to see why anxiety can be focused on dying and death. People in fear are aware that their hearts are palpitating or their breathing has become laboured, and these sensations often produce a further sense of panic that they are about to die. Death also figures frequently in anxieties because of its many fearful implications. In fact one psychoanalyst has said that every fear is ultimately a fear of death,[189] but this seems to be too great a simplification. Death is feared in that it means separation, loneliness, punishment, destruction, chaos and so on.[137, 205] Conversely any situation that threatens to bring separation, loneliness and the like can also arouse an associated fear of death.

The displacement of fear from sources such as these on to death is often seen in patients who seek help from doctors because they have recurrent panics in which they feel that they are about to die. It is useful to discover the original root of the anxiety. For instance, one rather shy woman in her early thirties went to her doctor because she repeatedly felt palpitations from her heart, each time thinking she was going to die. She later gave a relevant account of her personal life and feelings. She had an illegitimate child by a married man who eventually divorced his wife. The patient and this man had been living together and she wished to marry him in church. The priest refused to conduct the marriage but said that this decision might be reconsidered later if she ceased her present relationship with the child's father. Her wish to conform led her to return home to her parents, who disapproved of the man concerned and had not previously known of the illegitimate child. This troubled situation with desire and guilt in conflict made her very anxious, and she became frightened of dying. With treatment she came to understand and face the many factors involved in her troubled feelings and she made some readjustments in her way of life. Some natural anxiety remained, but the abnormal fear of dying receded.

An important aspect of death is that it forces people to part, and morbid fears are likely to arise at the prospect of the imposed and unsought-for separation. Yet again, feelings of personal unworthiness may give rise to a preoccupation over death or dying. These feelings were important in the case of a young woman who had through illegitimacy missed a normal upbringing, and also lost her foster-parent from heart disease. She grew up to be very unsure of herself, and felt she could never meet people on equal terms because of her illegitimacy. Whenever it seemed that she might come to like a person too much, she began to feel that the friendship might – or must – come to an end. Then she would be assailed by fears that either she herself, or the person she liked, might die. As is common, once her own anxiety caused her heart to hasten, the palpitations made her feel that her end was near.

Morbid fears of death can also grow rapidly in the setting of too possessive a love. Undue emotional dependence easily gives rise to a sense of resentment too disturbing to contemplate. It is distressing to feel angry, frustrated or irritable towards the person who is so needfully loved. In this emotional climate fears for the safety of the loved person can arise; there are torturing thoughts that the needed one will die, which seems to be the worst thing that could happen. Children not infrequently fear that their mother may die. The unusual degree of their fear is an indication of their disquiet over their own too great dependence. Psychoanalytic theories, based on the Oedipus complex, emphasize that a child must have some feeling of guilt over his intense love for his mother, a feeling that will induce fears of death.[24] Many do not agree with such concepts and prefer the explanation that the child's fear of his mother dying is an expression of his uncertainty in a bewildering world.

Alongside the fears of dying, people can be afraid that they might be seized by an overwhelming impulse to kill. Such recurrent, unwanted, illogical impulses and fears of killing or injuring are usually recognized to be foolish by the sufferers, but strive as they may, they cannot put them wholly from their minds. These feelings most often plague people whose normal outward behaviour is notably controlled, correct, and high-principled. They strive for fairness and are angered by cruelty and injustice, often setting themselves impossible standards. Yet these can be the victims of recurrent fears that they may impulsively kill someone who is dear to them.

Mothers can be very distressed by fears that they may impulsively harm or kill their own baby. Often they are women who feel that their own parents did not give them the love they needed. They lack confidence in their own ability to be adequate mothers, and on top of their other anxieties grows the fear of committing infanticide.[55] This not uncommon fear arose in one woman who was by nature somewhat nervous, sensitive and very house-proud. She had the recurrent fear of either killing her baby or herself. A previous child had died in infancy and she had been told that she was not trying hard enough during the delivery of her latest baby. In looking after her infant she met the material needs of her child quite adequately. At no time did she really want to harm him or kill herself, but the irrational fear that she might do this persisted for eighteen months until her depressed mood was relieved by psychiatric treatment. She had the same phobias for a short while when she next became pregnant.

The recurrent dread of having an irresistible impulse to commit suicide is not far removed from the common nightmare thought that many people have when standing over a chasm. There is the feeling that it would be possible suddenly to throw oneself forward. To those who are obsessed by such feelings, it seems that an uncivilized element of their nature has arisen to scourge them in the form of a fear of death or killing. In this context death is seen as an irrational enemy, within rather than without.

With so many sources of anxiety over death, it may seem that dying must be a time of fear. It is, of course, true that those about to die are influenced by their previous attitudes and fears of death, whether their ideas were normal or abnormal. It does not mean, however, that as they lie dying the most uncomfortable thoughts on death come to the fore. Often, fortunately, people reach a courageous serenity in accepting the inevitable that they did not gain during their lives. The fears that had formerly been displaced on to death frequently fall away again. Samuel Johnson was very perturbed by his long-standing irrational fear of dying, known to many of his friends. Boswell's tactless pertinacity on the subject had him so upset on one occasion that it threatened to end their friendship.[19] Nevertheless, at his death Fanny Burney could write of Dr Johnson,

I hear from every one he is now perfectly resigned to his approaching fate, and no longer in horror of death. I am thankfully happy in hearing that he speaks himself now of the change his mind has undergone, from its dark horror, and says – 'he feels the irradiation of hope'![27]

Death No More

As death is feared man would like to prevent it. He is also apt to regard himself as an exceptional creature with intellectual and moral stature that makes his death seem incongruous.[202] Except when he denies the evidence of his senses, however, man has the foreknowledge that he must die. In his struggle against death he can either attempt to defer it, or he can deny that death is absolute. It is of interest that in both these contexts life and death become linked with ideas of right and wrong.

Besides taking the obvious instinctive measures to safeguard health, mankind can defer death by forbidding deliberate killing, either of others or the self. This protection from death is mediated through world-wide ethical beliefs which ascribe to human life a sanctity, or at least a value, that inhibits its wanton destruction. In the civilized world departures from this principle are conspicuous, except in time of war, or when a society decides that certain other human beings have forfeited the right to live or even that some have never deserved the right to live. Measures to preserve life can offer only a brief pause, however, compared with the limitless promise of the belief in eternal life. This idea is again extensively bound to ethical concepts, the conviction, for example, that a worthy life on earth will contribute to a happy existence after death.

HOMICIDE AND SUICIDE

Killings are sometimes considered perfectly permissible and cause no ethical misgivings. This occurs more when social life is primi-

tive; the death of an acknowledged enemy is then purely a matter
for celebration, and the death of a stranger provokes no more than
some pleasurable fascination. Obviously civilized man is not so
very far removed from the savage in these feelings; both may show
little regard for the life of someone outside their own society, but
value highly their own lives and those of their companions. This
leads to the development within society of firmly held *mores* and
laws to prevent the killing of its members.

When the structure of civilization is secure throughout a large
community, death is only meted out in extreme situations. In so far
as people are united in a society, the death of any one is a loss to the
whole. For one of the group to cause the death of another jeopard-
izes the basis and ethos of the community. Murderous impulses
within the group threaten to dissolve its cohesion and must be
rigidly restrained and known to be so. People today profess and
largely believe that it is appalling to end the life of one of their
number. Such a killing is socially wrong; and the irrevocable step
of capital punishment for an offender against recognized principles
is the last and a fundamentally dangerous resort of society to
remove a threat to its integrity.

Nowadays, killing is sometimes pardoned or permitted, by both
general opinion and the law. Besides the excusable homicide that
occurs by accident or under great provocation, a society may
designate others as enemies, in war-time for instance, and permit,
encourage or even command their killing. Even those who
sincerely believe murder to be abhorrent may then kill and deny
that they have murdered. When the extreme threat to the community's existence has passed and peace is restored, society's rigid
demarcation between those to be attacked and those to be defended is lost. The conflict between the different ethical demands
fades, and men can once again wholly condemn the taking of
human life.

Most societies admire those who meet their death willingly and
bravely, but disapprove strongly of suicide. The attitude towards
suicide is complex.[190] People can be intensely hostile towards
those who attempt to kill themselves, if they think the reasons are
insufficient or cowardly. They may even punish survivors. Thus,

until 1961, people in England could be imprisoned for attempting suicide. There has also been strong religious condemnation of those who have killed themselves. Another legal requirement, until 1824, was that suicides be buried at the cross-roads with a stake through their heart. The rulings forbidding burial in consecrated ground and demanding the forfeiture of the suicide's goods were not relaxed until near the end of the last century.

On the other hand, there have been certain times and occasions when suicide has not been condemned and has even been approved. It has been called altruistic suicide by Durkheim, a sociologist.[45] Societies have permitted or approved of people killing themselves when shamed or irretrievably insulted. The captain could go down with his ship or the Japanese commit *hara-kiri*. In primitive societies there have been three circumstances when suicide has been condoned or even forced upon a person by social pressures. These were the suicides of women on the death of their husbands, followers and servants on the death of their chief, and old people when senility had made them useless.

Suicide may occur in our culture when people can no longer tolerate their life or themselves. Sometimes their decision seems justifiable. More often it is because they are seriously depressed, and the thought that life is no longer worthwhile often comes to them unbidden.[119] Those who suffer intense misery may only avoid suicide because they judge it to be wrong. This moral reluctance to end life is supported by a realization that it would hurt those who love them. Even in their unhappiness they may view suicide as an act of cowardice that would only pass on problems to others.

Restraining thoughts and religious injunctions may prove insufficient, and unhappy people do attempt and sometimes succeed in ending their lives. The tragedy becomes even greater when a seriously depressed person kills members of his own family first, in the belief that it will save them from worse harm. It is often a doctor's duty to save the lives of those who have attempted to kill themselves – most suicidal attempts do not end in death. This assumed medical duty can be questioned, especially when the patient's future seems an undeniably poor prospect. Nevertheless, the vast majority of those whose suicidal acts are not fatal leave hospital glad that they are living. Without any external constraint they make no further attempt to end their lives and may later wonder how they came so near to killing themselves.

ETERNAL LIFE

The better ordering of society may prevent some untimely deaths but cannot, of course, ward off death for ever. Most societies, however, have comforting beliefs that temporal life on earth is but one aspect of total human existence. In prehistory this view appears to have been held; at the burial of the dead, companions often placed objects beside the body, presumably thinking that these gifts could still in some way be used or appreciated by the dead person. For instance, the skeleton of a Neanderthal man was found interred in a hollow in a cave floor at La Chapelle-aux-Saints in the south-west of France. Alongside the body had been placed the leg of a bison with flesh still attached.[115] This bit of ritual – a symbolic declaration that the dead man still had some needs and was not utterly finished – probably took place about seventy thousand years ago, during the last glacial period.

During man's evolution the rituals of burial became very elaborate among the many societies that evidently contained in their culture firm beliefs in an after-life. Some Bronze Age barrows contained the dead, fully dressed and wearing their ornaments; the men had their weapons to hand, and beside them were pottery vessels with food and drink.[73] Besides believing that the dead required such necessities for their new existence, burial objects indicate that the living have often imagined that the dead would undertake a journey, frequently across water. Some graves in Egypt contained ships or were in the form of a boat. Pieces of gold have been placed in the mouth of the dead with the express purpose of providing a fare for the ferryman to take them across the river to their rightful place with the dead. The Viking boat-graves could contain alongside the corpse all sorts of riches, weapons, tents, sledges and animals, sufficient for the spirit to make a voyage and then live elsewhere.[181]

The material splendour of the graves and, presumably, the

materialistic ideas of the needs of departed spirits, have attained
ghastly levels of elaboration. The excavations at Ur of royal
graves nearly 5,000 years old showed that a king or queen might be
accompanied to death by all the members of the court. Woolley
described the uncovering of a royal tomb to reveal, first, the bodies
of five men, then ten carefully dressed women, then a chariot with
the remains of two asses and the grooms, then more bodies,
riches weapons and tools. Before the king's body was located the
death-pit revealed further soldiers, wagons, grooms, court ladies –
a total, in all, of sixty-two people in the pit and a further three
persons with him in his chamber. It appeared that the victims
walked to their appointed places and perhaps took some drug
which produced sleep or death before the final burial.[213]

The cult of the dead took on extraordinary importance in
ancient Egypt, with an extensive provision for the life after death.
As far as possible the dead bodies were preserved. For those of
importance there were elaborate tombs and even the massive
pyramids. A regular supply of provisions was thought essential
for the dead in their continuing existence. Mortuary priests and
their successors were bound to supply fresh food, supposedly in
perpetuity, otherwise the dead suffered from starvation and
neglect. Later it was accepted that models rather than real objects
would suffice for the dead. Illustrations of hunting, harvesting and
the like would allow the deceased to participate in such necessary
and enjoyable activities in the after-life.[46]

These various observances during or after the disposal of the
dead emphasized the belief in a continued, perhaps grander, life
elsewhere, once mortal life was over. Many cultures have myths
that express a slightly different view of the possibility of continued
existence. These contain beliefs that once upon a time man did
not die, that there was a Golden Age, or an innocent eternal life in
a Garden of Eden. The present loss of immortality is thought to
have come about by chance or by misdeed. There are numerous
tales that ancestors could renew their life by changing their skins
or taking a secret medicine.

A myth from the Melanesian culture of New Guinea relates that
in the primeval past, when people led their existence in the nether

world under the ground, individuals growing old, grey and wrinkled would rejuvenate by sloughing their skin. This ability was retained when people first lived upon the earth, but then it was lost. The story tells of the olden times, when, as was the custom, an elderly woman went out of sight of others to become young again. She swam off a little way and discarded her aged skin, but on her return she was not recognized by her granddaughter, who became frightened and drove her away. The aged woman recovered her old skin from the water and resumed it. From then on this power was lost to man, ageing and death were inevitable, although animals 'from below' like snakes and lizards still retain the power to change skins. When these people of New Guinea die now, they leave for the spirit world, although they are visited by the spirits of the living mobilized during sleep or trances. Gifts, messages and information can be passed from the living to the dead in this way. At a special annual feast the spirits return to visit their villages, which make suitable preparation.[126]

These beliefs in different forms of spiritual existence for the dead – and for the living – that were reported from New Guinea have parallel forms in many primitive cultures. Examples from Indonesia and Africa have already been cited in the previous chapter, where it was noted that the spirits of the dead were occasionally to be feared by the living. Usually, however, the spirits of ancestors are revered. They are thought to be essentially just, bringing benefit to those who lead a good life. They have their own mode of existence; the Yoruba in West Africa, for instance, believe that the spirits of the dead men become grouped with other ancestral spirits according to lineage and town. They will eventually be reincarnated.[136]

Many take comfort from a belief in eventual rebirth after death, with the promise that death only interrupts life, and that there will be a return to the wanted familiar world. This view of a constant rhythm of life, death and rebirth is the keystone of several religious beliefs, primitive or otherwise. It is in accord with the natural cycles seen in this world, like the succession of the seasons and the annual regeneration of plants. Not everyone is comforted by a prospect of recurrent life in this world without surcease, however.

Men do not necessarily want to be condemned to endure repeatedly the pains and uncertainties of this life. Plato believed that the philosopher who was temperate and inclined to the contemplation of eternal values would, after death, have his soul liberated from the flesh and live in bliss with the gods.[168]

The belief has similarities to the views of Gautama, the Buddha. After his own renunciation of a princely inheritance, Gautama taught awareness of the illusory value of earthly struggle. All life is suffering, caused by craving; so suffering can best be ended by the annihilation of craving. Unless nirvana, with the peaceful end of worldly desire, can be attained, there is condemnation to an endless cycle of craving, existence, birth, old age, death, ignorance, and again, craving. Death, in this context, is only a further condemnation to the transmigration of the soul and continued existence. Nevertheless with a life of patience, humility, abstinence, respect for life and morality, one might approach more nearly nirvana and the end of life and of death.

Ideas of immortality in Judaeo-Christian beliefs have followed a different path. Some very early conceptions from the Middle East are indicated in the Epic of Gilgamesh, that remarkable written record probably contemporary with the royal tombs at Ur.[172] The cuneiform characters on the clay tablets refer to the hero's encounter with an underworld life which contrasted with the true immortality of the gods. Such myths evolved so that towards the end of the Old Testament period there was a growing belief in the possible resurrection of the dead to an existence more akin to life as we know it. This immortality was linked with the Judgement of God and the idea of a final resurrection at the end of time.[186] Christ was the 'first-fruits'.

THE REWARD OF HEAVEN OR HELL

If our society wholly accepted traditional Christian beliefs, there would be a general conviction that death was vanquished. In fact, in England about a quarter of the population disclaim any religious belief and about a half do not believe in an after-life.[69] This is not very different from the results of studies of opinions in the U.S.A.

When a number of people were asked what death meant to them, although many replied that it would be the beginning of a new existence, rather more spoke of it as the end of life.[52, 53]

This trend has been increasing over the last few decades; a comparison of student attitudes in 1935 with those of 1970 demonstrated that, although they now admitted to more frequent thoughts of death, there was less belief in life after death.[118] Even in older people, when thoughts on death seem more pertinent, the majority have no conviction of life eternal. In one investigation the views of two hundred people over the age of sixty were gathered by presenting them with a number of selected statements that had been made about death, and then asking them which views they agreed with. Less than half, 45 per cent, of these elderly folk viewed death as the beginning of a new and better life.[193]

Current atheism or agnosticism is not the whole explanation of the lack of assurance concerning future life. Although many religious people find comfort concerning death through their faith, not all with religious belief are reassured. It was even found in one study that those with religious beliefs had more fears of death than the non-religious.[54] A convinced belief in a future life by no means eradicates anxiety over death. In one respect this may be because many naturally anxious people seek certainty in religion, yet remain anxious. The other explanation is that religions do not usually hold out unconditional promises of pleasurable eternity even to those of their faith. The faithful must observe certain moral codes during life on earth. By doing this they have the prospect of eternal bliss, but the wayward may face future punishment after death. Sometimes the standards of ethical attainment are set so high that the ordinary individual cannot but despair over his shortcomings and consequent failure to merit immortal reward.

This doctrine has been stressed by some in popular Christian thought; it can be better taught and understood than the conception of an eternal world metaphysically different from the sensible world, with its illusions and trivialities. Although the importance of a moral life on earth to existence after death has been preached, there is no simple guarantee of eternal heaven for those who lead

a good life and hell for those who do not. In fact, Christian
doctrine has asserted that man is a guilty sinner and deserves the
punishment of death.

St Anselm in the eleventh century firmly and succinctly attributed human death to human error.

Moreover, it is easily proved that man was so made as not to be
necessarily subject to death; for, as we have already said, it is inconsistent
with God's wisdom and justice to compel man to suffer death without
fault, when he made him holy to enjoy eternal blessedness. It therefore
follows that had man never sinned he never would have died.[7]

St Thomas Aquinas expounded further the accepted view of St
Augustine: God's will is paramount. By mortal sin man has
forfeited eternity and merits eternal punishment. God is not the
cause of sinning, but he leaves some in sin and gives 'grace' to
others; those in 'grace' who persevere in good are delivered from
sin. Nor did Calvin bring any liberal comfort to Christians.
Although some were the elect for heaven, the predestination of
others, regardless of their life on earth, was condemnation.

The horrors of death have been emphasized by moralists to
encourage men to mend their evil ways. Artistic representations
from the Middle Ages show death as a malignant, skeletal figure
with scythe, hour-glass, sword, fatal darts and the like, cutting
down man in his vice and folly.[68] There was a recurrent theme
contrasting the Three Dead with the Three Living, the latter
generally pictured in their vanity as kings or other holders of
earthly powers.[207] Morality plays also impressed the power of
death upon those who needed warning to cease evil-doing.

A neutral picture of death was not considered sufficient to
convert the unbeliever. To encourage the spiritual laggards there
have been terrifying portrayals of death and damnation.[184]
Death has been depicted as a loathsome figure of decaying flesh
with its skull-like head bearing a sadistic smile, hell pictured as
full of suffering and torture. The patient in his death-bed has
often been regarded as a particularly suitable subject for demonstrating the necessity of the church's religious guidance. The
medieval *Ars moriendi* was a religious treatise that illustrated

legions of horrible and persuasive demons increasing their
insidious assaults on man as he weakened in his last illness.
Demons offering crowns were opposed by angels exhorting the
dying to humility and indicating the benefits of Christian faith.

Such images must have provided powerful incentives to belief
for the simple, impressed by the power of the church, or for the
dying, whose thoughts were expected to turn to God and the
repentance of sins. Rousing the fear of death and damnation
persists as a technique for conversion. Revivalists seeking converts
have induced a mass feeling of dissatisfaction, guilt and fear in
their audience before suddenly holding out the hope of religious
salvation. John Wesley, when he preached of damnation to turn
people from sin, rejected Swedenborg's description of hell because
it was said to contain just red-hot ashes and not everlasting fire.[195]

In present-day Britain such fierce convictions are rare. Only
half of the population believe there is an after-life, and their
conceptions of it do not conform very closely to any religious
viewpoint. In fact, recent theology cannot easily give uniform,
simple guidance on immortality in view of present scepticism
about bible mythology and the current trend to revise ideas on the
after-life.[187] In Gorer's report of the religious views expressed by
the laity in 1950, only one person in eight spoke of the judgement
and the possibility of hell.[69] Most saw the after-life as heaven or
peace. They thought that perhaps there would be some reunion
with their loved ones, or perhaps they would watch over those still
living. A few thought there might be a reincarnation.

Gorer's more recent inquiry into current views of eternity
showed what mixed views are commonly held.[70] The belief that
eternal life after death is determined by conduct on earth is
fading. Individual fantasy of the after-life appears to hold greater
sway than religious teaching. Although this means that during
life fewer fear the possibility of eternal hell after death as a
deserved punishment for sinful ways, equally the religious belief
that this life is a preparation for the next has been diluted almost
out of existence. Increasingly few, it seems, are protected from the
fear of death by the belief that it is not an annihilation, but the
beginning of a fuller life.

4   Acceptance of Death

Many people are able to accept, without undue disquiet, the fact of death, refusing to ignore it or to deny its finality. Their acceptance is based on an understanding of its nature that is never complete. Even the early stage of appreciating the inevitability of death does not come too easily to the young, the primitive or the reluctant. Usually, however, childhood experiences and learning soon bring some realization that death means an end to life. The developing ideas about death expressed by children may sound naïve, but often this is only because they voice with artless conviction the poorly integrated, tentative views that adults do not so readily reveal. Some people never gain much insight into death; a few reject the idea of natural death and explain death's coming in other ways that they find more acceptable.

COMPREHENSION OF DEATH

The evolution of the ideas that children hold about death has been studied systematically by Nagy.[138] She examined carefully the compositions and drawings on the theme of death produced by nearly four hundred school children in Budapest. She also talked to them individually, getting them to speak of the ideas they had expressed in their writings and drawings. Children under five years did not recognize death as final; it was seen more as a sleep or a departure. Life and death were not mutually exclusive, a person could be 'very badly killed'. Some children thought dead people remained alive in the grave, growing and knowing what was going on. Others thought of people dying and soon becoming angels. Nagy was impressed by the recurrent theme of death as separation, which seemed most significant to these young children. Over the age of five, the children showed an increasing awareness that people did die. Death was seen as a being, a frightening one, often a skeleton or a white shape. The child could also think of death as a dead body, being unable to distinguish these two concepts. After nine years or thereabouts children accepted that life ended in death, but they commonly held the belief that there was a soul which lived on.

The English children whom Anthony studied seemed to show a similar pattern of developing comprehension.[8] At about seven or eight years of age, she found that children advanced considerably in their understanding. They began to appreciate that people died and associated this with such themes as burial, killing, lying horizontal and hospital treatment. After eight years, children could say more about the biological essentials of death and realize more what was meant by 'not living'.

Although even the child can soon understand in theory that life on earth must eventually end in death, the actual coming of death to a known person is not so easy to accept. Killing often seems to be better understood than death, unless it is a death occurring in extreme old age. This also applies to some primitive tribes, notably the Trobrianders and Bushmen; although well acquainted with death in the world about them and among their own community, they may yet deny the existence of natural death. Information from many studies of different primitive societies has been brought together by Simmons to show the patterns and trends of their beliefs about death and their behaviour towards the aged.[182] Of forty-seven tribes, seventeen did not regard death as natural, twenty-six admitted the possibility of natural death and four tribes recognized frankly that death might come from natural causes.

In some ways it seems strange to deny natural death, by preferring to believe that the manner and time of death is the machination of some enemy or some power. However, men commonly wish to blame others rather than acknowledge their own ignorance or personal limitations, and if they cannot admit that their own natural and inevitable death is inherent in themselves, they may find it easier to denounce someone or something for bringing about undesired deaths. When a member of a primitive community dies, then his fellows wonder if it was due to poison, or sorcery, the work of an evil spirit, or the malevolent inspiration of an enemy.

In both primitive and civilized existence there is the recognition that life must end some time. It is usual for the tribesman explicitly to blame a malign agency for the death, but civilized people are also apt to blame others following bereavement. An example of this sort of attitude has been described in the New Guinea tribe of the Arapesh, a friendly people living in the mountains. The death of one of their number would be attributed to the machinations of the distant plainsmen. Placing the blame on outsiders also prevents ill-feeling within the tribe.[128] The Yoruba of Nigeria have been inclined to attribute the visitation of death either to particular gods, who therefore need propitiation and sacrifice, or to witches.[136] Like Europeans not so long ago, they have been apt to blame elderly, childless women for working witchcraft. Innocent old women thought to be witches became scapegoats for the deaths, especially untimely deaths, of others. The bereaved could even punish the 'witches' for their supposed evil-doing. Although such beliefs can to some extent make the coming of death more acceptable, they become less necessary when people believe that it is wholly fitting for life to end.

TIMELY DEATH

To see death as entirely appropriate (an important part of much religious teaching) removes misgivings. It also has firm support from biology. When a person has completed his span of life, his powers wane, and the eventual increasing decline indicates that it is time for the individual to depart this life.

There is some biological immortality. It is more lasting than the short-lived remembrance of the deceased in the society to which he belonged. For a while personal memories and influences may linger and perhaps a lifetime's achievements will endure rather longer, but firmer assurance that personal life does not utterly perish depends upon the individual's children. The elderly get comfort when they see their children and perhaps their children's children continuing in this life. They are links in a potentially immortal chain. Within the living bodies are the chromosomes, inherited from parents and ancestors and capable of infinite replication. Once the individual has safely passed on this genetic endowment he has contributed to his immortality. In accordance with much that goes on in nature, however, he himself need survive no longer. It is egocentric to hope otherwise.[184]

This biological necessity to die has influenced some of the psychological concepts of man's nature. Jung thought that anyone who regards death as a meaningless cessation and not as a fulfilment of life's goal, alienates himself from his own instincts.[97] Some psychoanalysts have gone further, postulating that there is a death instinct. It may seem paradoxical that man, who so often shows an urgent instinctive striving to live, can have an instinct towards death, but this was suggested by Freud. It came rather late in the evolution of his psychological principles, in 1920.[58]

Freud suggested that to counterbalance the drive for self-preservation and reproduction, there could be an instinct towards death. Together, these two instincts would preserve the rhythm of creation, living and dying. The mortal portion of the individual could pursue its course to death once its racial function was over. The polarization of life and death instincts has also been woven into psychodynamic explanations of human behaviour, as determined by an equilibrium between opposing drives. It has been postulated that the death instinct may be concerned in more than the progress of an individual towards his inevitable death. It could be an intrinsic part of the destructive and aggressive drives against others and against the self.[59] A culmination of death instinct directed towards the self would be suicide.

Whatever the explanation, death does appear to be more acceptable to the aged. Some elderly people speak of their own deaths almost with indifference.[145] Other people who are fond of an elderly person are not quite so distressed by the thought of his passing, since he has reached old age. In some cultures there is a marked contrast between the private regret and grief at the death of a young person and the public celebrations following the death of an old person who has completed life and achieved all that could be desired.[136]

The death of the patriarch has often been a time of honour and worship, a climax to a useful life. The words and actions shortly before death have been regarded with respect or even veneration. A person approaching the end of life might even hold back important advice or counsels until they could most suitably be announced. The last statements of the Maori, for instance, were considered unbreakable testament, an example of the widespread respect accorded to the statements of the dying. Any blessings or curses uttered by the dying have been accorded great significance. The approach of death could be a time of magnificent and awe-inspiring abdication of power, when worldly goods were granted to the deserving and authority bestowed.

The deaths of elderly people in some primitive societies came about in an accepted form very different from this. In hunting or herding nomadic tribes, which have to keep on the move if they wish to survive, there came a time when the aged person who could no longer play an active role was an impediment to his people. In many tribes it was accepted by all that this was the occasion for the old person to be left to die; it was not accounted cruel or ungrateful but the necessary end of a formerly useful life. Even the Hopi Indians, with their respect for the elderly, excluded those who became helpless. When this stage had been reached the old and frail were mortally neglected. The Omaha would leave the enfeebled behind at a camp site with shelter, food, water and a fire while the rest moved on. This hastening of death for the old has been a world-wide custom, practised by about half of such nomadic tribes whether they be North American Indians or Eskimo, Lapps or Bushmen, Ainu or Australian aborigines. It has been less common among settled peoples, fishers or farmers. As cultures grow more stable and complex, with fully established laws and religion, accelerating death for the aged becomes rarer and is finally condemned.[182]

In primitive society the elderly have not necessarily waited for natural death or the decision of their companions that the time has come. The aged in Samoa might make the request to be buried alive, the traditional method employed. It would be considered a disgrace to the family of an elderly chief if this honour were not granted.

When an old man felt sick and infirm, and thought he was dying, he deliberately told his children and friends to get ready and bury him. They yielded to his wishes, dug a deep round pit, wound a number of fine mats around his body, and lowered down the poor old man into his grave in a sitting posture. . . . His grave was filled up, and his dying groans drowned amid the weeping and wailing of the living.[203]

In some societies the elderly candidate for death took an active interest in the preparation for his dispatch. Indeed, the arrangements could include a feast at which he was guest of honour. His part then came to its anticipated abrupt end.

SEEING DEATH WITHOUT FEAR

Death may also be accepted for the unhappy reason that life is felt to bring more pain than pleasure, and this negative welcome of death as a long-lasting ease to life's fever is not rare. One in ten of the elderly patients that Feifel interviewed regarded death as a relief or a sleep.[54] Many of the adults who answered the questions in the Mass-Observation survey spoke of the burden of life; they were condemned to be themselves and only the sleep of death could commute this.[145] The majority of those whose lives have contained major practical handicaps and problems battle on without hankering after the final surrender to death. It is those who are discontented with themselves, dissatisfied with the routine of their lives and frequently exhausted by their own emotional conflicts, who think of the peace that death might bring. The apparent acceptance of death is often spurious, however. Although they may often feel that death's ease would be welcome, it would be a peace at the price of failure. Their wish for surcease from the struggle, which is based on a desire for greater fulfilment in life, could not be answered by the fiasco of dying. Although the rest from turmoil might be welcome, death would leave so much undone, so many ambitions unfulfilled. Only if all hopes are surrendered, will despair make death and failure acceptable.

The sad fact that some people pursue lives so desolate and troubled that they can look on death as a relative haven, contrasts with another approach to death. There have always been people who are prepared to give up their lives because they hold something in life greater than their own death. Martyrdom for religious faith may be rare now, but there are occasions of social strife, disaster and war when people deliberately accept death. The following quotation comes from the diary of a Kamikaze pilot, one of the Japanese volunteers who flew their load of destruction into the enemy target:

I am actually a member at last of the Kamikaze Special Attack Corps. My life will be rounded out in the next thirty days. My chance will come! Death and I are waiting. The training and practice have been rigorous, but it is worth while if we can die beautifully and for a cause.[88]

There is little doubt that the early volunteers for this patriotic suicide were enthusiastic, almost ecstatic, in their willingness to sacrifice their lives. Initially there was hope that by destroying the American aircraft-carrier force their sacrifice could turn the tide of Japanese defeat. Some of the later Kamikaze pilots, who had lesser hopes of victory and were subjected to greater pressure to volunteer, had a period of melancholy on joining the 'special attack' units. After a short while, Nakajima claims, they usually became involved in their mission and experienced spiritual calm. Morale was undoubtedly high in these volunteer units; they were jealous of their privilege to offer their lives as an inevitable sacrifice. Exctracts from their letters home show this.

Cadet — was dropped from the list of those assigned to take part in the sortie, upon my arrival. Cannot help feeling sorry for him.
Please congratulate me. I have been given a splendid opportunity to die. This is my last day. The destiny of our homeland hinges on the decisive battle in the seas to the south where I shall fall like a blossom from a radiant cherry tree.

Such ecstatic faith can evidently overcome all the doubts and fears about death. Often coupled with such fervour is a belief in predestination that also eases the prospect of dying. If, for example, the Mohammedan firmly believes that his life and death, his joys and grief are already ordained, then he need not fret because neither struggle nor distress can alter the immutable.

Many thoughtful men and philosophers, without relying on overwhelming religious values, have encouraged their fellows to accept that they must die. Men should not blight their lives with misgivings over its end. Montaigne, for instance, affirmed that death should neither be ignored nor unduly feared.

The end of our race is death; 'tis the necessary object of our aim, which, if it fright us, how is it possible to advance a step without a fit of ague? The remedy the vulgar use is not to think on't; but from what brutish stupidity can they derive so gross a blindness? They must bridle the ass by the tail. . . .
We trouble life by the care of death, and death by the care of life, the one torments, the other frights us.[135]

Such sensible opinions from a vigorous Christian will gain approval from those with no belief in any future existence, but they already have their own champions. Three centuries before Christ, Epicurus insisted that man should look steadfastly at the prospect that life's end was complete and he need not be troubled by hope. The popular concept of epicurean philosophy – to eat, drink and be merry – was graphically presented at feasts by passing around models of skeletons or corpses in coffins, coupled with exhortations to the feasters to enjoy the day. Epicurus himself gave cooler advice. Like Plato he insisted on the necessity of correct modes of thought but denied the more popular promise of life after death as a reward. He argued logically for the total acceptance of death.

Become accustomed to the belief that death is nothing to us. For all good and evil consists in sensation, but death is a deprivation of sensation. And therefore a right understanding that death is nothing to us makes the mortality of life enjoyable, not because it adds to it an infinite span of time, but because it takes away the craving for immortality. For there is nothing terrible in life for the man who has truly comprehended that there is nothing terrible in not living. So that the man speaks but idly who says he fears death not because it will be painful when it comes, but because it is painful in anticipation. For that which gives no trouble when it comes, is but an empty pain in anticipation. So death, the most terrifying of ills, is nothing to us, since so long as we exist death is not with us; but when death comes, then we do not exist. It does not then concern either the living or the dead, since for the former it is not, and the latter are no more.[49]

Such a creed does not bring easy comfort and only a minority will be able to accept it wholeheartedly. Epicurus himself appears to have lived according to his teaching.[168] In a letter, said to be on the day of his death, he wrote:

On this truly happy day of my life, as I am at the point of death, I write this to you. The diseases in my bladder and stomach are pursuing their course, lacking nothing of their usual severity; but against all this is the joy in my heart at the recollection of my conversation with you. Do you, as I might expect from your devotion from boyhood to me and to philosophy, take good care of the children of Metrodorus one of his first disciples, who had died·.

Other philosophers have also shown by their conduct that their words on the matter of life and death have not been empty. It is said that Spinoza, who had stated that 'A free man thinks of nothing less than of death, and his wisdom is a meditation not of death but of life', showed no sign of emotional distress on the day of his death.[168] It may seem that only an exceptional person could show such saint-like courage and calm as death approached, but the next chapters, concerning the way that ordinary folk die, will show that this is no rare virtue.

The Dying

Mortal Illness

Most of us at some time or other wonder about the way in which our own lives will end. How long are we going to live? Of what will we die? Can fatal illness be diagnosed with certainty? Is it absolutely inevitable that even if we avoid fatal accident or disease for seventy or so years, from then on an inherent process of ageing will gather momentum until it brings about our death? As yet there can be no definite answers or unqualified reassurance for such questions, but some reply can be given in terms of probabilities and possibilities.

LIFE EXPECTANCY

Each year a wealth of statistical data is published about the life, health and death of people. The facts gathered by the Registrar-General for England and Wales indicate that a boy born now can expect to live sixty-nine years; an average girl baby would have a longer life, seventy-five years.[162] This figure of life expectancy is only a theoretical guide, of course. It is a statistical manoeuvre expressing how long the average baby would live if exposed throughout life to the currently prevailing circumstances influencing health.

The attainment of seventy years by the average person is comparatively recent. It has been estimated that in Roman times the average life expectation was twenty-two years, in the Western civilization of the eighteenth century it was thirty-six years, in 1910 it was fifty-two years for men and fifty-five for women.[111] In the last hundred years the average length of life has increased enormously. Changes of this nature have taken place throughout Western civilization; for example life expectancy may be a year or so longer in Australia or Denmark than in Britain, which in turn has marginally greater figures than the U.S.A.[117] In previously less well-developed countries with a high mortality especially amongst infants, recent changes have made dramatic alterations in life expectancy and the population has expanded in an unprecedented way.

It may seem somewhat paradoxical that life expectation has only recently reached seventy years, when the biblical estimate was the same. It means that nowadays the average man is very likely to achieve this allotted life span, whereas in former days the lives of the majority of people were shortened by injury or disease. Taking the Registrar-General's figures for 1969 it is possible to see that a high proportion of men and even more women now survive to old age. If a group of baby boys were to live their lives in the circumstances of the present day, 98 per cent could be expected to survive the somewhat hazardous first year, 91 per cent would still be alive at fifty years, 80 per cent at sixty years, 55 per cent at seventy years and as many as 23 per cent at eighty years. Girls can expect a longer life: 73 per cent would be alive at seventy years and 45 per cent at eighty years.

Social and medical advances since the beginning of this century have enabled many more people to reach the age of fifty years. But once that age has been reached, modern conditions have not been so successful in further prolonging life expectancy. The fifty-year-old man in 1911 could expect about another twenty years of life. Half a century later this had only increased to about twenty-two years. It is a meagre advance, which reflects our comparative failure to make much headway in the prevention or cure of the serious diseases and deteriorations of middle and old age.

CAUSES OF DEATH

What are these killing diseases which are so common and yet we seem relatively powerless to control? They are the cardiovascular disorders, cancers, and diseases of the lung such as bronchitis and pneumonia. More than one person in three dies from a disorder of his heart or the blood vessels supplying the brain. About one person in five dies from cancer or a similar malignant condition. Among men in England and Wales, about two fifths of these fatal cancers now originate in the lung, and this particular form of the disease we largely bring upon ourselves. Other diseases of the respiratory system end the lives of one person in eight. The remaining fatal disorders play a far smaller part in the overall mortality. The various forms of violence grouped together only account for one death in twenty-five.[162]

Each stage in a person's life has its own particular pattern of fatal hazards. In childhood, the first twelve months are the most vulnerable period, but infant mortality has reached a very low level in Britain with 982 of every 1,000 infants born alive surviving their first year.[162] The incidence of congenital malformations apparent at birth has not decreased, however, and remains a problem. Children aged one to five years hold on to life more firmly. The number of deaths of children of this age in 1960 was half that of 1950, an impressive fall. Acute infectious diseases used to bring death frequently, especially to younger people. With increased knowledge and general fitness many infections have now lost their menace. The death-rate from diphtheria in the 1930s was 290 per million. In 1955 it was 1 per million. The figures for measles, scarlet fever and whooping cough show a slightly less dramatic fall, but nevertheless there has been a tremendous decline in their death-rate. The much more effective treatment of tuberculosis has made a large contribution to the lowered mortality in childhood. Older children have considerable viability. Although it may seem incredible to parents, children from five to fourteen years of age have the lowest mortality rate of any age group.

During the three decades from fifteen to forty-four years, there is a relatively low but steady toll of deaths, largely due to fatal accidents and a few cancers. Towards forty-four years of age however, coronary thromboses begin to become a not uncommon cause of death. These years of adolescence and early adult life are the ones for which most has been achieved. Tuberculosis is far less likely to kill; in 1950 over 1,600 young people between fifteen and twenty-four years died from tuberculosis, but by 1960 the comparable figure had fallen right down to only twenty-eight deaths. It is less good to learn that deaths from violence increased in the same age group by half. The motor-cycle contributed to this: 110 young men died from motor-cycle accidents in 1950, 450 were killed in 1960 and the figure has risen a little more since then.

After forty-five years of age, the more familiar pattern of mortality is established. Cancers and diseases of the circulatory system begin to take their heavy toll of life and from then on do not slacken this levy. From forty-five until sixty-four years, one third of deaths are due to cancer. From sixty-five years onwards, disorders of the vascular system end the lives of an increasing proportion of people. Cancers and similar malignant conditions still prove fatal only too frequently, but a breakdown of efficiency in the heart or blood-vessels kills many more. This is especially so for people who have lived more than seventy-five years – and it is to be remembered that now two-fifths of the population do live to that age. We seem to be able to do little more than touch the fringe of the problem of the circulatory disorders at present.

These few figures, selected from the many available, give the expectations of the 'average' person in Great Britain: how many years he can expect to live and the sort of disease most likely to end his life. Other factors can be taken into account to make a more accurate prediction for a particular person. The sex, occupation, place of dwelling and so on, may all tend to differentiate the individual from the overall 'average'. Women live longer than men. Their increased viability becomes apparent from forty-five years of age. During the succeeding twenty years their mortality rate is practically a half of that for men. The married person is less likely to die than a single person of the same age; this difference is most noticeable in earlier adult life. It may be due, in part, to the disabled person being less likely to marry, as the same disability which deters from marriage may lead to premature death in the single state. This is not the total explanation however. Some of the acute fatal conditions, including violent deaths, are commoner in the unmarried.

Living conditions can alter the likelihood of developing fatal disorders. Even in a comparatively small geographical area like England and Wales, the mortality rate varies between different parts of the country. For instance, there is a higher mortality rate for those living in the North. On the whole, mortality is higher in towns than rural districts, although Greater London is favourable in this respect. Deaths from bronchitis play a considerable part in the increased urban risk. The manner of life associated with differing occupational groups influences mortality. Death tends to come a little earlier to those in the lower classes of the Registrar-General's classification. The difference is clearer if the particular occupations are taken into account, rather than the broader divisions of social class. Miners, for instance, tend to have shorter lives, teachers and clergy have longer.[35, 163] There is some variation in the types of fatal illness for people in different social classes. Coronary heart disease is more common in higher social classes. Cancer of the stomach and bronchitis are more frequent causes of death in lower social classes.

So far the fatal disorders have been referred to by their diagnostic labels. They all bring about death by interfering with one or more vital functions of the body. In vascular disorders the blood supply to an organ may be increasingly reduced or stopped abruptly by the blockage of an important artery. In strokes the brain is damaged by an interruption of its blood supply. If particular parts of the brain cease to function, unconsciousness and death follow. Cancers can kill, by growing into the tissues of vital organs and destroying their normal efficiency. Besides the immediate damage from their spread, they may interfere with general nutrition. Acute infections may kill by damaging one or more parts of the body or by the general spread of toxic products. Respiratory diseases, perhaps with often-repeated infection, can destroy the lungs' vital task of transferring oxygen into the blood and removing carbon dioxide. Kidney diseases, such as nephritis, can not only interfere with excretion of waste products but start a sequence of bodily changes that may end in death from the consequences of high blood-pressure. Near the end of life a number of vital processes will often decline rapidly together.

DIAGNOSING FATAL ILLNESS

Although it becomes obvious that an ill person is dying when it is seen that some failing vital function is past recovery, it is not always easy to be certain earlier on in the illness that the condition is fatal. Of course, it is important for those responsible for the care of patients to know if recovery is likely, so that they can consider fully how best to help a seriously ill person. If those in charge of a mortally ill patient are unduly reluctant to concede the fact until his dying breath, both the patient and those who feel for him may have had to endure more hardship and uncertainty than they should. On the other hand, if illness is too readily diagnosed as incurable some patients will suffer through the resultant *laissez faire* attitude leading to neglect of early opportunities of treatment, and some will endure unnecessary mental anguish by mistakenly anticipating death in the near future.

The recognition of fatal illness is often only too easy. The signs and symptoms may be such that a doctor will know straight away that his patient is dying. For example, it may be clear that a person has a malignant form of cancer which has spread hopelessly far and wide over his body. In other cases a fatal illness may be suspected and after some straightforward investigations the disease and its eventual outcome are known for sure.

Uncertainty usually arises either because the diagnosis of the disease is not fully established or because it is not clear what course the disease will follow in a particular case. Gross mistakes in the diagnosis of fatal conditions are not common. They can occur, of course, but do not often arise when the disease is fairly advanced. One patient, whom I visited during an inquiry into the experiences and needs of dying people, had been admitted to hospital in a very poor condition after he had coughed up a lot of blood. He had been given radiotherapy for a lung cancer without having much benefit from the treatment. The haemorrhage occurred during a visit to London, and it looked as though he would never return home. In fact, it turned out that he had an unsuspected tuberculous disease of his lungs that could be cured by the appropriate treatment.

Such reprieves by truer diagnosis from seemingly fatal illnesses become increasingly rare with modern levels of diagnostic skill. The problem the doctor usually faces is not often the one of being quite confident of such a diagnosis and then being proved wrong, but of being uncertain of the exact diagnosis and having to decide how far to pursue the matter when it appears from a patient's general condition that he is dying. Some diseases can only be diagnosed beyond all doubt at the expense of considerable risk or discomfort for an ill patient. It is not easy to strike a balance between unremitting investigational zeal for diagnostic minutiae, which may make a patient's remaining days a misery, and a restraint which accepts some uncertainty but could occasionally be judged neglectful.

Another common cause of uncertainty in prognosis is the unpredictable powers of recovery that seriously ill people may show. There may be a valuable even if temporary improvement from, say, severe heart disease. Occasionally patients may make a quite unexpected spontaneous recovery from conditions that are nearly always fatal; for instance, some people with invasive cancer have made mysterious extensive improvements. In the more chronic conditions there is the slender chance that a new effective treatment may be discovered before the patient dies. In recent decades a number of diseases have ceased to be death warrants. The diagnosis of diabetes, pernicious anaemia, and tuberculous meningitis, for example, do not carry the same degree of sinister import that they once did, and, when the new treatments were discovered, some 'dying' patients were reprieved.

There are no universally agreed criteria which can always separate patients with a fatal illness from those who will live on. I doubt if there can be; but in practice there is sufficient medical knowledge for reasonable certainty in nearly all cases – provided those concerned are not prevented from using their judgement by an emotional reluctance. Even though there are no explicit rules, when those experienced in caring for seriously ill patients consult over any particular case, they usually come to an easy unforced agreement regarding the broad plan that balances the needs for further investigation, treatment and general care.

DEATH FROM OLD AGE

The potentially fatal diseases are, to some extent, comprehensible. There remains a greater mystery: Is there some inherent process that dooms man to die after a certain number of years of life? Is there a natural life-span?

These questions now seem of greater importance because of the more frequent part that senescence plays in the deaths of our present-day population, with its greater proportion of elderly people. It has not always been so, nor is it universally so now; famine, poverty, plagues, and violence have often cut short the lives of so many, that an individual's hope of long life has been slender. Such times of hardship and strife resemble the struggle for life in some animal species, where ecological studies have shown that in the wild state increasing age may have little adverse effect for the majority of individuals compared with the disadvantages of youth and inexperience. Lack has shown in the robin, for instance, and in other species of wild bird, that once the first few very hazardous months are over, death comes almost equally to younger and older individuals.[107, 108] Robins in captivity may well live more than ten years, which would be rare in the wild. To the robin, secure in his cage, senescence is more likely to be important in bringing about his death; perhaps it is analogous to man in his civilization.

In attempting to answer some of the questions concerning senescence, ageing and life-span, the basic data are often peculiarly difficult to obtain. Fact, exaggeration and myth become almost inseparable when information on longevity is sought, but Comfort's review of ageing processes disentangles relevant knowledge and hypotheses.[41] Tortoises appear to hold the record with life spans of more than a hundred and even one hundred and fifty years. In mammals there is some correlation between longevity and the ratio of brain to body, so that species with relatively large brains tend to live longer. Man is the longest-lived mammal, with a few authentic records of more than one hundred and ten years and one reasonably certain life of a hundred and twenty years.

There does appear to be a limited span of life in man, so that survivors into old age die through an inevitable deterioration of their health. Senescence may be estimated for a population by actuarial methods which can demonstrate statistically the increasing liability to die with advancing age.[129] This concept of senescence is not identical with the idea of a recognizable process of physical deterioration. The term senecsence is perhaps more commonly used in the non-actuarial sense to describe the apparent and suspected bodily changes with failing functions in the ageing individual. There are two important sources of this deterioration. First, there is the accumulating damage of past injuries and diseases which have left their mark on the body. Second, there are the apparently innate bodily changes coming with old age.

The accumulation of damage to the body does appear to be the main cause of senescence in some lower vertebrate animals. In higher animals, notably mammals, it appears that these scars are by no means the whole explanation of the ageing process and more important is the second cause, the intrinsic changes which make the individual visibly old with a less tenacious hold on life. In theory the first-mentioned cause of senescence, the legacy of life's buffeting, might account for senescence in man. The decreasing proportion of people left alive with advancing age could be due to the steady attrition of disease and injury. As the death-rate increases rapidly in people after they are seventy, however, rather than rising uniformly with age, it would seem likely that there is some process that comes into play or accelerates as the seventies are reached. It also parallels the ordinary observations of man's ageing. Athletic prowess is lost comparatively early; mental agility lasts more years but then noticeably declines. Fertility diminishes, ending abruptly in women. Youthful comeliness is lost with the changes of bodily shape and posture, with hair growing grey and thinning, skin becoming wrinkled and so on. As such changes of failing vitality become more extreme, death from 'old age' is anticipated.

Theories about the processes of ageing are only very tentative. They are of particular interest in that they might lead to methods of delaying the progress of senescence and deferring death. Some of the theories explaining senescence are based upon the progressive failure of human cells to continue to multiply efficiently and replace the normal steady loss. In experiments some tissue cells can be kept alive and growing outside the body. They appear to be able to propagate with perfect cell reproduction for an apparently limitless period. In the body of man cell multiplication may become progressively inefficient. Microscopic examination of the chromosomes has shown increasing mistakes in the 'copying' process.[93] This could possibly be related to some inherent property of body cells which determines that they can reproduce a large but nevertheless limited number of times. Perhaps an enzyme system fails. It is also possible that there is accumulating damage from toxic substances collecting in the body. The radiation to which we are inevitably exposed may have a cumulative effect. There is no shortage of hypotheses to explain why the cells of the body may not reproduce properly, but confirmation of the theories is either non-existent or, at best, partial.

Another contribution to the body's deterioration with age comes from the complete failure to replace certain specialized cells when they are dead. If cells are badly injured or suffer a serious disease process, they die. Although many cells are then automatically replaced, in some organs no similarly functioning cell will be substituted, only scar tissue. The nerve cells of the brain are like this, irreplaceable. When important tissues are lost in this way, the failing function may have a direct effect on health. Also, the failure of one organ or gland may indirectly cause other tissues to deteriorate and function imperfectly.

A further possible explanation of senescent body change is that the materials which are used to construct cells or their surrounding matrix themselves may deteriorate. The very complex molecules of proteins and other essential body components may not be reproduced sufficiently exactly. Then, although apparently normal, they would not function as well. Colloidal materials, it has been suggested, are particularly liable to mechanical or chemical changes in the body.

At present, there is no good indication that any particular one

of these hypothetical causes of senescence will prove to be correct.
Nor is it immediately foreseeable that such a basic cause of ageing
could be altered. There is some reason, however, for not regarding
the time of onset of the senescent changes as entirely immutable.
For instance, certain pure-bred species of mice have a predictable
expectation of life; but if two selected lines are crossed, it is
possible to obtain offspring which live considerably longer than
either parent. This phenomenon of heterosis has been observed in
several species.

Another now well-established observation on rats has given
rise to hopes that it may eventually prove feasible to defer human
death for a while. It has been possible to extend the life of rats,
even doubling their expected age, by selective restriction of their
diet as the young rats grew.[132] Limiting the calorie intake of the
diet, but providing all the other necessary constituents, slowed
growth for long periods, even up to the whole of the normal life-
span. If the diet was then unrestricted, further growth took place
and the animals still lived a long while, with a great increase in
their total longevity. Of course, it must not be assumed that this
experiment can even theoretically have any direct application to
man, let alone practically. Body growth in rats and men is by no
means identical. It does provide, however, a pointer to further
researches.

How does death come about through senescence? The bodily
changes of old age could, in theory, lead to gradual failure from
tissue deterioration until life just stopped. Usually, however,
there is some immediate cause that precipitates death. Sometimes
the deterioration of an essential organ like the heart or brain
reaches a crucial point, so that any further worsening brings about
a crescendo of disorders in many parts of the body. It often seems
that in later life the tide of illness can be dammed back no longer.
Weaknesses can be patched for a while, but another wave of
disease comes and resistance disintegrates. Careful post-mortem
examinations of the elderly have often shown the presence of a
number of chronic conditions.[30] Perhaps it would be as well not
to accept too readily that the deterioration in old age is just
'ageing'. There may be covert, long-standing diseases slowly

pursuing their course and reducing vitality before finally bringing about the death of an affected person, a death in old age.

All the important inquiries into the physical roots of the alterations of old age, whether they be ingenious animal experiments, investigation of small cellular changes or search for unrecognized disease, should not blind us to the social factors contributing to senility. It is common experience that elderly people playing a necessary part in the world carry their years lightly. Perhaps their physiological responsiveness and resistance to disease may parallel their liveliness. The apathetic unwanted soul who finds life a miserable existence seems to succumb to illness too readily. It is known that when elderly men again find useful roles, as they did in wartime, they are less likely to kill themselves,[171] but this is a highly selective feature of the socially determined influences on mortality in the aged. In a more general way, may have seen an elderly person apparently rejuvenated as he finds a new interest or new part to play in life. Vigour returns and resistance to illness appears to increase. The same changes may be seen in a hospital geriatric unit where morale is high and the elderly are encouraged to be active. The sequence of biological changes which cause people in favourable circumstances to lose this burden of years is debatable. We must remain aware that a social assumption that elderly people are senescent can contribute to their decline.

Our greatest hope is to extend the period of enjoyable and useful life. Certainly only a few would think it a gain to prolong life if it meant an extended period of senescent existence with further deterioration ever encroaching. Though death can perhaps be deferred, no one wants to lengthen the process of dying.

6   Physical Distress in the Terminal Illness

Dying is often feared as a possible time of physical distress, and although death can often come without discomfort, sometimes this concern is quite justified. Reassurance is often sought about three aspects of dying – will it take a long time to die; is it likely that there will be severe physical suffering; will this be relieved? While attempting to answer these questions in turn, for the sake of convenience, it is obvious that these aspects of possible suffering in the last illness cannot be kept separate from each other. Severity, duration and the chances of full relief from distress are inter-related. A severe pain that only lasts moments when sudden death brings an abrupt halt to life has different implications from an equally severe pain persisting or recurring over a long period. A mild degree of discomfort that can be easily borne for a few days may utterly wear down a person over months. Of itself, the fact that the terminal illness goes slowly may be advantageous rather than terrible. An elderly contented person, who is well looked after, may experience little or no discomfort – only a slow, gentle loosening of the demands of life and the wish to live. A fatal disease can be present for years, lying quite latent or only causing minor changes; meanwhile life can be lived to the full or with minor well-compensated handicaps. Such a long period with an incurable but not immediately fatal disease would be a bad prospect if it entailed suffering.

THE DURATION OF THE TERMINAL ILLNESS

Most fatal conditions come in between the extremes of sudden catastrophe and long, lingering illness. In a recent survey one death in ten was considered to be unexpected, generally due to some vascular disorder.[36] Fatal diseases often end with a period of illness during which there is no prospect of any worthwhile improvement before death – a time of serious restrictions, loss of independence and, perhaps, discomfort.

Much of the available information on the course of fatal illness is biased towards more chronic disease, where there is time to collect data and it is necessary to provide care for the dying patients over a period of time. An idea of what can happen in one form of sudden death is given in the recollections of people whose hearts had been restarted after cardiac arrest while they were receiving treatment in hospital.[44] They could be said to have died and yet been revived. Some patients remembered the event. They described 'going into nothingness', 'fading out like lights', 'feel forced to pull your mind back to your body' or 'as if your bones are rubber'. One person overheard a voice saying 'My God, his heart has stopped' and remembered thinking he could not be dead as he was still breathing.

The majority of deaths are not so sudden and, in Britain, often involve a period of time in hospital, perhaps in a ward for the chronic sick or for geriatric patients. Even with relatively chronic conditions, the terminal illness does not last so very long. It was reported in a national survey that 75 to 80 per cent of mortally ill patients died within three months of their last admission to hospital.[87] This was similar to the finding in a rather more detailed investigation in just one particular geriatric unit, where 82 per cent of those with fatal illnesses died within three months of admission.[51] For these elderly patients the terminal, potentially painful, part of the illness averaged about six weeks if they had a fatal cancer. Those who were crippled by arthritis or bone disease suffered much longer. They might be ill and severely handicapped for months or years before their condition led, indirectly, to their death.

Although the figures quoted apply to the very large number of chronic fatal conditions, there are many patients who die in hospitals which cater for patients with more urgent disorders.

I have obtained comparable figures for the patients who died in a teaching hospital during 1962 and 1963. The policy in these hospitals is usually to favour the admission of patients with acute conditions and there is a lower proportion of chronic sick and elderly patients. As expected, it proved that patients who died in this sort of hospital had a considerably shorter terminal phase to their illness. As many as 10 per cent of those whose condition proved fatal died on their first day in hospital and altogether 30 per cent of the deaths happened within a week. Seventy-five per cent of those who were to die in the hospital died within a month, and nearly all, 97 per cent, of the deaths took place within three months.

The nature of the fatal illness made a considerable difference to the length of the terminal phase, of course. Approximately a thousand patients died in this teaching hospital during this two-year period. The swiftness of the various fatal conditions is indicated by the percentage of patients who died from the different diseases within one week of entering hospital. On the whole it was the sudden serious disorders of blood vessels that killed most quickly. Seventy per cent with fatal strokes died within the week. Fifty per cent of fatal coronary thromboses brought death within a week. Forty per cent of the other deaths due to heart or vascular disease took place within the same period. In fact, 40 per cent of all other fatalities except those due to cancer occurred within seven days of the patient entering this hospital. Incurable cancers did not usually give such a brief terminal phase, but even with this condition 20 per cent did die within a week of their last admission to hospital.

The statistics quoted from different kinds of hospitals are a guide to the length of the last phase of the mortal illness, but they may mislead. They will underestimate the length of the terminal phase if the admission of patients to hospital has been delayed. Moving very ill patients to hospital and altering their familiar routine may itself hasten the end, especially in some elderly patients. For instance, although there is no comprehensive report to tell how swiftly death comes to those admitted to homes for the dying, in one such home 56 per cent died within the week of

admission. They must have been admitted at a manifestly terminal
stage.

These figures only represent the terminal phase of illness in
hospital and those who die at home could possibly follow a somewhat different course, a factor to be remembered in that more than
half of the deaths in Great Britain take place out of hospital.[87]
Even in this country, with its easy access to hospitals, many die
without any consultation or treatment from hospital staff during
their last illness. It is possible that they tend to have dissimilar
symptoms in their last illness or even to be slightly different
people from those who readily come to hospital. Even with a
disease like fatal cancer, it was recently reported from Sheffield
that no less than 9 per cent of patients never attended hospital
for treatment. Either they did not wish to go, or it was recognized
that their condition was so far advanced that hospital treatment
had little to offer that could not equally well be given at home.[210]

The data from a Chicago report on many aspects of the care of
cancer patients shows that the progress of patients at home did not
differ so much from those in hospital.[89] The length of the period of
terminal care was similar for patients at home and in hospital.
The average was about three months, although the illness had been
recognizably present for an average of seventeen months. The
different types of cancer tended to progress at different rates.
Cancers of the lung or digestive organs usually rendered people
seriously ill for nine or ten weeks before death, whereas malignant
growths of the skin, mouth or throat might involve a considerably
longer period of unpleasant symptoms.

In Great Britain there are some figures for cancer patients who
were cared for at home and not solely in hospital. A group of
lung-cancer patients, who were initially treated in a London
hospital and were later visited at home, were not bedridden for a
very long period. The majority were confined to bed for less than a
month and 10 per cent needed more intensive nursing for only a
few days.[11] A recent report from Sheffield of cancer patients whose
terminal care took place in their own homes showed that half the
patients died without any period of difficult nursing. Only 15 per
cent of this group of patients needed such intensive care for more

than six weeks. Unfortunately, quite a few of the 15 per cent had a troublesome time for twelve weeks or more.[211]

The 1972 study conducted by the Institute for Social Studies in Medical Care assessed how long people had severe restrictions placed on their lives by the fatal condition.[36] Two thirds had some restrictions for three months or longer, especially those over seventy years of age. One person in six was either largely or totally confined to bed for at least three months. People who had been in a hospital or institution for over a year before they died were not necessarily confined to bed and the period of greater limitations or recognized terminal illness could well be only a few weeks or even none at all.

It is hard to draw any firm, simple conclusion from these diverse data, collected from different sources in various ways and with the terminal phase of an illness often difficult to define. I hope it will not be too vague or misleading a summary to say that although a small proportion are struck down suddenly and a small proportion have months of being seriously ill before they die, the majority will have a terminal period requiring special care lasting a few days or week and not usually exceeding three months.

PAIN WHILE DYING

Pain is the symptom that many people commonly fear will be the dreadful accompaniment of their dying illness. It may indeed be an inherent part of some incurable diseases but it is by no means inevitable. Moreover, few people in this culture are allowed to follow the 'natural' course of a distressing mortal disease.

First, it should be acknowledged that it is not easy to assess with any great accuracy the intensity of pain felt by troubled, dying patients, especially when they are chronically ill. This does not imply that a doctor will overlook the pain of seriously ill patients, but that detailed knowledge of the exact quantity and components of their pain sensation is not so easily gained. Doctor and layman usually have slightly different problems in evaluating people's pain or distress. The doctor wishes to make a valid assessment so that he can use the best means of bringing comfort to his patient. The layman is unsure how much someone is suffering and can be greatly perturbed that a very ill relative could possibly be in pain without others being fully aware of this or doing enough for it. Distress is a subjective symptom, something that is felt, and therefore very difficult to define and impossible to measure accurately. If all discomfort, including mild aches, were accounted distress, it might lead to over-treatment of symptoms with powerful drugs or the use of other extreme treatments which involved more discomfort or risk than the original trouble. If, on the contrary, an observer errs the other way and regards pain as distressing only where there is gross undisputable evidence of agony, then the seriously ill may bear the brunt of this underestimate of their discomfort.

Although we usually think of pain as an unpleasant sensation it is not necessarily accompanied by distress. To some extent pain is just a sensation like heat or cold though a further emotional feeling is usually inseparable from this sensation.[74] A considerable amount is known about the stimulation at the sensitive nerve-endings and the conduction of impulses in the nerve fibres, but rather less about the function of the brain which translates these messages into what we feel.[100] The relationship between the nervous system and the mind in respect to pain is very complex.[21] For instance, one person may be distressed by the pain from a bruise that another person ignores. Moreover, a bruise that a person might experience as mildly painful at one time, he might find most distressing when morale is low, or not even notice when thoroughly distracted.

This influence of the state of mind equally applies to those with severe disease or injury. This was shown in the case of a woman who had a recurrence of a cancer some while after most of the original growth had been removed. This spread to involve the nerve roots to her leg and gave her pain, so that she needed to re-enter hospital. There was no effective treatment for the growth and she was given drugs to relieve the pain. It was planned that she should return home, but then the pain worsened and, even with frequent injections of morphia, she was still distressed. It was clear that she could not manage at home in such a state and arrangements were made for her to be transferred to another hospital, where she could remain for the rest of her life. As soon as she learned this she was greatly relieved, because she had been convinced that she would not receive adequate care in her rather lonely home. As her anxiety settled so did her pain, and she did not need nearly so much of the analgesic drugs.

When morale is high or the prospect hopeful, conditions that ought to give rise to the sensation of pain may cause remarkably little distress. A dramatic example of the relationship between pain and emotion was observed among troops at the Anzio beach-head. Beecher, an expert on the assessment of pain and the pharmacology of drugs relieving pain, found that only a quarter of the severely-wounded men wished for anything to relieve pain. These wounded were quite conscious and had not had analgesics for some time, if at all. This lack of distress from pain was psychologically determined, perhaps in great measure due to the relief experienced by men at their release from an intolerable experience.[16] At a more everyday level, a study of patients' experience of pain in hospital has shown that their complaints were influenced in a significant, although complex, way by the nature of their relationships with the nursing staff. Given a setting of easy, confident communications, seriously ill people made fewer complaints of pain requiring relief.[18]

In most surveys of mortally ill people, when significant pain is reported, it usually refers to a degree of pain that distressed the patient. This implies that the pain is such that even with aspirin or similar remedy the patient is still troubled. One of the earlier estimates of the discomfort of the dying was made by the renowned physician Osler at the beginning of this century. He gave a succinct summary of the frequency of physical discomfort in the dying, mentioning that in five hundred patients in their terminal illness, he found 18 per cent to suffer some bodily pain or distress.[146]

In a more recent report on a group of elderly patients who died in a geriatric ward, 14 per cent had pain which was not adequately relieved.[51] The experiences of these older patients should help dispel any disproportionate fear that death from cancer is inevitably painful. Although a quarter of the patients dying of cancer were liable to pain, in all of them it could be controlled by regular and, if need be, powerful doses of an appropriate drug. This liability to pain did not usually go on too long, on average about six weeks. Exton-Smith, who cared for these older patients, quotes Saunders' experience in the hospice where she and the nuns care for the dying. The fatal illnesses were less often painful in the elderly, about a fifth of those over seventy being liable to pain, which was half the prevalence of pain younger dying people might experience. However, in the patients admitted to this hospice, with proper care and avoiding unnecessary parsimony over drugs, it was always possible to control pain in terminal cancer.[173, 174] Exton-Smith found the greater difficulty was to control the pain in the elderly patients who were crippled by arthritis and similar disorders. These patients with very painful chronic diseases could not so readily be given strong narcotic drugs, and yet their diseases caused them to be bed-ridden and were the indirect causes of their death.

In a group of patients I visited during their fatal illness in a general hospital, two thirds were liable to experience pain which required treatment for its relief.[80] This potential suffering was a little more frequent than in a comparable group of other patients with severe illnesses that were not fatal. The big difference was that the non-fatal illnesses were soon rendered comparatively painless, while 12 per cent of all those with incurable disease continued to suffer some pain in spite of the treatment they received. Unfortunately, regular visits and reports of these dying people could only confirm that in some the failure to achieve adequate relief of pain did persist. In those who remained conscious (unconsciousness mercifully protects many from suffering towards the end of life) about one person in eight continued to have pain for some part of the day. At times they had a mild degree of discomfort that did not trouble them much, but it was likely to get really painful at other times. A few were rarely free of pain, although it had been dulled. This proportion of about one chance in eight of experiencing pain in the terminal illness seems to be a fair generalization from the various sources. It seems to be more common than it should be.

It is not easy to discover the proportion of those dying at home who have much pain. To some extent the problem is dealt with by admitting the distressed to hospital. It is those who need hospital care and do not get it who may well suffer a great deal. Once again, much of the information available is concerned with the needs of cancer patients during their terminal illness. Perhaps it should be interpolated that in this book, concerned with dying, cancers are spoken of as frequent causes of death; but a very considerable proportion of cancers are treated successfully and cured, so that health and the expectation of life are unaffected.

The district nurses who provided the reports which were the basis of one survey found that of seven thousand cancer patients, over two thirds had moderate or severe suffering.[94] This was not only physical pain however, with which we are mainly concerned at this part of the discussion; it is the combined figure for both mental and physical suffering. It is a most disquieting report, nevertheless. In another report on the terminal care of cancer patients at home, their relatives were subsequently asked if the patients appeared to have enough sedation and relief from pain. It seemed that about a fifth of them had physical distress that was not relieved, and almost another fifth had a lesser degree of discomfort.[2]

The investigation described by Cartwright and Anderson enquired from relatives of the needs of people during their last year of life. They reported that two thirds of the patients had a distressing degree of pain at some time, in fact it was the most frequent symptom. Fortunately, pain was again shown to be helped more readily than many other symptoms and nearly ninety per cent obtained some relief.[36]

OTHER PHYSICAL DISCOMFORTS

Pain is not the only symptom to plague the dying. Other symptoms such as nausea and vomiting can make the dying person feel wretched. Vomiting can be caused by many different sorts of diseases and occurs quite frequently when the kidneys or liver are ceasing to function adequately. It can also be due to an obstruction of the alimentary canal. If the obstruction is high up, swallowing may be so interfered with that most food or even liquids will not go down. Attention to diet, anti-emetic drugs and, when suitable, operations to relieve obstruction, will often relieve these symptoms of nausea, vomiting or impaired swallowing. They are not as easily controlled as pain, however; in one group of dying patients who experienced nausea and vomiting, only about two thirds gained adequate relief with treatment.[80]

Breathlessness is a serious source of distress to the dying. It can become extreme when failing lungs or heart will no longer respond to treatment, and it is hard to endure. There may be episodes when the most laboured breathing seems ineffective and, indeed, this may be the moment of death. These are not the same as the panicky periods of over-breathing experienced by people with a morbid fear of dying. The patients nearing death who survive these awful moments of fighting for their breath may later describe the sense of suffocation, and the feeling that they were about to die. The remark of one man who had experienced this severe breathlessness during the night – 'I don't think I could go through that again' – was a sentiment many have felt. Fortunately these acute attacks can often be relieved by morphia.

The breathlessness experienced by those who have a slowly encroaching disease of the lungs is not easily relieved. All of us who knew one young man, dying from chronic lung infection and asthma, were very troubled by his state. He had many treatments over the years, all the obvious ones and some of the heroic. Over four years he had been in and out of hospital, increasingly breathless. For the last three months of his life in hospital he was helpless, as any effort caused him more distress, even when he was given additional oxygen. His comments were brave, but showed how he felt, while we were impotent to give any lasting practical help: 'The breathing's no better – I wish I were striding out to work'; and, after a very breathless few days, 'I was quite aware of being on the brink of passing on, but I didn't'.

The feeling of malaise or exhaustion is difficult to define but is real enough to those whose existence is pervaded by the feeling of being very ill. The accumulation of lesser discomforts which have gone on a long while and the sense of ill-health can mount up to cause a total distress that can be more difficult to relieve than acute pain. Of two dying men in a ward, one with a cancerous invasion of bone which could cause severe pain and another dying of cancer of the oesophagus which was not painful, it was the latter who seemed to suffer more. The first man, with a well-defined cause for pain, had this symptom effectively relieved. The second endured more from the cumulative effect of less urgent symptoms like nausea, cough, difficulty in swallowing, hoarseness of voice and a profound sense of weakness. One does not wish to paint too gloomy a picture, but these other symptoms are not rare. Eight per cent of the previously mentioned group of elderly dying patients were found to be distressed by physical symptoms other than pain.[51] In the general hospital group it was as high as 19 per cent.[80] Many more would have had these serious physical discomforts were it not for treatment.

In brief it appears that much of the physical distress of patients dying in hospital can be alleviated, but not all. With good care, the pain of most fatal conditions, including cancer, can usually be relieved. The breathlessness from failing heart or lungs too often remains an unsolved problem in the terminal phase. The other forms of physical distress can often be alleviated but are liable to cause continued suffering. In general, it can be said that unless the care is exceptional, about a fifth of patients dying in hospital are apt to endure a distressing amount of physical discomfort for an appreciable portion of the time.

The discomfort experienced by people dying at home can differ from that of hospital patients. In the absence of immediately available skilled professional care, physical discomfort may not be dealt with at once and distress can soon develop. Home care is not always enough to cope properly with the cleaning and dressing of open sores and ulcers, which may then become more painful. When bladder or bowel fail to function properly in hospital patients, some help is soon at hand and extreme discomfort can usually be avoided. Away from this immediate source of treatment and nursing skill, retention will give rise to pain and incontinence can cause discomfort as well as shame. Colostomies, where part of the bowel is short-circuited to open on to the front of the abdomen, can be a nuisance at first – although nothing like the anguish that would arise if the obstruction remained unrelieved. Soon after operation, soiling from the colostomy seems difficult to prevent, the bowel acts irregularly and people with a recently constructed colostomy are conscious that they can easily get unclean and smell. After a while, colostomies usually settle down to function regularly and cleanly without giving rise to further difficulties.

None of these things are a bar to home care, only to inadequate home care. When patients are well tended in their homes, they may benefit a great deal through spending all or a greater part of their last illness in familiar surroundings. In the Chicago survey of cancer patients at home and in hospital, only about a quarter of the patients with cancer came to need special nursing care at the terminal phase.[89] Some were troubled by unpleasant odours and disfigurement that developed in their terminal illness, but the incidence of these disturbing accompaniments of the advanced cancer was not as high as is often feared. This study reported that for more than half of the cancer patients their suffering was limited to the feeling of debility with some degree of pain; and the pain, it appeared, was usually relieved.

AGE AND EASE OF DYING

The age at which people die has some bearing on the amount of physical suffering that they experience. Younger adults tend to have longer-lasting illnesses, often with greater physical distress. In the patients dying in hospital, 45 per cent of those under fifty years of age had considerable discomfort; 32 per cent of those dying between fifty and seventy years old had physical distress; but only 10 per cent of those over 70 years had much unrelieved physical suffering in their terminal illness.[81] The older person tends to slip away from life a little more easily.[36] The younger person, perhaps because of his better general health apart from the fatal condition, survives rather longer and endures more. To some extent modern medicine has tended to prolong terminal illness; many of the superimposed infections and complications which formerly curtailed the course of terminal illness are now curable. Pneumonia no longer comes so often as the 'old man's friend', allowing him a swift exit. Nevertheless older people still tend to have less distressing terminal conditions.

The type of fatal disease does, of course, influence the distress experienced by the dying. Some diagnoses have a worse reputation than others, not always justifiably. The most frequent causes of death in old people are the disorders of the heart and circulation, and the cancerous diseases. Cardiovascular disorders may cause little or no distress if they give rise to a swift death from a coronary thrombosis or a stroke. If, however, there is a long process of narrowing arteries with increasing symptoms as the disease encroaches on the function of different parts of the body, patients can have a hard time of it. Cancers are not the worst causes of death in terms of distress, although if the necessary help is not obtained, they can be cruel. The almost universal fear that cancers are long, terrible, implacable diseases, although occasionally true, is often belied by the peaceful end that they bring. Quite often, especially in the elderly, who have other troublesome diseases that are incurable, it is not the fatal disorder that brings most of their discomfort.

The extent to which a person suffers physical discomfort during his last days also depends upon how conscious he is. In most terminal illness, varying according to its nature, the majority of people become increasingly drowsy and eventually are unaware of what is happening to them and around them. It is hard to say if the early impairment of concentration does or does not ease physical distress. If there is just a little confusion, it is possible for physical discomfort to become magnified in the mind, which senses some loss of control. More usually this lessening of awareness is kindly; the remembrance of recent discomfort fades, perception is a little clouded and the immediate future is not so full of the sharp awareness that pain may return. In the later stages of the mortal illness, full awakening with alert concentration becomes less and less common. Quite a few have little appreciation of their last week of life. Sometimes this is due to drugs, but frequently it is inherent in the progress of the disease. In hospital, a third of the patients knew nothing of their last day of existence and only 6 per cent were conscious shortly before they died.[80]

The moment of death is not often a crisis of distress for the dying person. For most, the suffering is over a while before they die. Already some of the living functions have failed and full consciousness usually goes early. Before the last moments of life there comes a quieter phase of surrender, the body appears to abdicate peacefully, no longer attempting to survive. Life then slips away so that few are aware of the final advent of their own death.

7 Emotional Distress in the Terminal Illness

The ways in which people tend to react as death approaches become familiar to those who take part in caring for them. Often the emotions of dying people evolve into an acceptance that they are about to die. Most finally meet death, which they may have formerly regarded with anxiety, grief and awe, in a manner that compels admiration. Nevertheless, mingled with the courage and the varying degrees of acceptance of the inevitable are a host of other emotions, pleasant and unpleasant, some concealed and some plain for all to see. When people are gradually dying, their mood is not often wholly constant. Optimism and pessimism, stoicism and fear can easily follow one another. Sometimes the mortal disease directly affects the function of the brain so that the dying person acts quite out of character. Possibly I shall dwell too much upon the unpleasant emotions and give an unduly sombre picture, but it is important for those concerned with the dying to be aware of the distress that can occur so that they can play a part in relieving it. For the sake of convenience anxiety is discussed first and then a number of unhappy feelings are grouped under the heading of depression.

ANXIETY

It is reasonable enough for any seriously ill person to feel very worried about himself. Much of our behaviour towards the dying is based on a feeling that the dying person is bound to be even more fearful about himself if he knows he will not recover. There are

few reports of the actual frequency of anxiety in these circumstances however. Osler's report, early in this century, stated that
11 of his 500 patients were apprehensive in their last illness.[146]
This assessment of only 2 per cent of dying patients showing
anxiety appears to be a lower figure than most people find. The
percentage who show anxiety will depend, of course, upon the
closeness and the duration of the observation. This particular
comment that Osler made was based upon the routine reports of
the attendant staff. If closer inquiries are made into the emotions
of dying people, a greater number are likely to tell of their fears.
A psychiatrist who quite recently held more detailed interviews
with a small number of dying persons found anxiety to be more
common than had been mentioned in this early report.[32]

A considerable proportion, 13 per cent, of patients dying in a
general hospital were observed by the nursing staff to be obviously
anxious.[80] These were the patients I came to know, and besides
finding ample confirmation of anxiety in those who were obviously
uneasy a further 25 per cent spoke of their considerable apprehension or described frequent periods of distressing fear. They
also showed the betraying signs of emotional disquiet, looking
tense and fidgeting, with the facial expression and demeanour of
anxious people. Of course, anyone seriously ill in hospital has
cause to be worried owing to the potentially bewildering or
frightening experiences of hospital life, the separation from home
and so on, but comparable patients in the ward with non-fatal
illnesses were clearly less apprehensive. It seemed evident that,
whatever the reason, mortal illness was a more potent source of
fear. The anxieties of the dying tended to fluctuate from time to
time, but there was no definite trend to become more fearful or
less fearful as the illness progressed. Some became a little more
anxious in the last week or two of life, that is, if drowsiness did not
intervene. Others changed from being apprehensive into a more
steadily courageous frame of mind, acquiescing in the inevitable
progress towards death.

What are the causes of anxiety? There is the apparently inherent
fear of death already discussed. Nevertheless, anxiety is by no
means restricted to those who acknowledge that they may be

dying; in fact, anxiety seems about equally common in those who recognize that their lives may be about to end and those who apparently do not. It is often impossible to be sure which particular aspects of the situation of the dying cause their fear. Sometimes the reasons for anxiety seem clear enough and it is easy to have intuitive explanations of why the dying should have misgivings, but intuitions can be fallacious. Can we be in equally accurate sympathy with the person from an altogether different walk of life or the dying child, the aged widow, the woman with a painful illness, the paralysed man formerly proud of his strength and so on?

Given a chance, most dying people are only too willing to tell anyone prepared to listen what it is they fear. Frequently it is the possibility of severe physical discomfort – that it may become intolerable or that some very painful symptoms they have had may return or continue unchecked. One ill man said that he could hardly contain his panic at just the thought of again having to go through the sort of pain that he had suffered at home during the few days before he came in hospital; and as he spoke he was tremulous and suffered from recalling the recent memory.

When breathing is affected an elemental fear is soon aroused. A patient with a tumour in the chest had found it very difficult to breathe when the growth had increased in size. Most of his breathlessness was then relieved by radiotheraphy, but he was not entirely free of it. He was a brave man, but on days when his breathing was rather more laboured, he was very anxious. Fear does occur more frequently among those dying of diseases that affect their breathing – in the general-hospital patients two thirds of those who were breathless experienced anxiety, whereas only about one third of those with other discomforts such as pain were as fearful.[80] Several spoke of their distress of mind due to their struggle to breathe; it is well recognized by doctors who care for incurably ill patients that those dying of heart disease, troubled by the struggle for breath, often become fearful and agitated.[51]

There are other consequences of the fatal illness besides discomfort that bring anxiety. Severe illness will often bring about a separation of the patient from his friends and relatives, just at the time when he most needs their comfort. This effect may be more

obvious or more remarked upon in children, although it certainly
is not confined to them. In one group of fatally ill children who
were being treated in hospital, their fear often arose when they
were separated from their family. This was more noticeable in the
younger ones under five years of age. Anxiety was not only due to
separation, of course. The children, especially those from five to
ten years old, also showed fear of painful experiences, some talking
of their dread of possible future pain. The slightly older children,
usually from ten years and upwards, showed more anxiety and
depression over the deaths of their fellows. A few even spoke of this
matter and the possibility of their own death. Even though the
younger children did not show so clearly the apprehension over
dying, the doctors concerned detected signs of such anxiety, but
it was largely overshadowed by the fear of separation and painful
procedures.[140]

It is not always easy to tell the main source of a dying person's
fear. It is quite a normal phenomenon for people to concentrate
their conscious worrying on to a minor source of anxiety because
the major fear is too overwhelming to think of. The anxiety can be
displaced on to a lesser symptom, so that a patient will seem to be
making a lot of fuss over, say, a stiff joint when he is dying from a
disease he dare not consider. It is not unusual for a very ill person
to feel more upset about another person in the ward than he is
about himself. A man who was unlikely to recover from his chest
disease said that he was not one to let his condition trouble him.
Yet, while speaking of this, his eyes filled with tears and he became
very tense as he mentioned a near-by patient who had just been
readmitted to hospital very ill with a similar disease. 'I can't help
feeling sorry for him. He's terribly worried about his family. He
was so pleased when he went out.' Although these apprehensions
about the other patient troubled the equally ill speaker, he did not
confess to any anxiety for himself. He would not think of it.
Incidentally, this is one of the problems that face patients in a ward
with other very ill people. They can less easily escape entirely from
the thought of serious disease and its consequences when they are
confronted with others with similar problems; they tend to feel it
is the presence of the others that upsets them.

Anxiety does occur more commonly in those with a long terminal illness. This was shown among the patients dying in the teaching hospital. Less than a fifth of those who had been ill for under three months were apprehensive. As the months of illness increased the incidence of anxiety became greater so that more than half of those who had symptoms for over a year were anxious.[80] As a fatal disease progresses, the causes for feeling troubled can mount up and each of them may be a sufficient reason for the dying person to feel anxious.

It would be useful to know what sort of people are more prone to be anxious when dying and what conditions are most often linked with fear. As yet there is no known infallible guide to indicate who will be frightened during his last illness and who will show little anxiety. The feelings of any one individual cannot be accurately predicted, although there is often an intuitive feeling of how well a person may adjust to the awareness of dying. For instance, an actress never given to reticence over her emotions throughout her life, did not spare the rest of the ward when she was troubled during her last illness, except on the occasions when she retired under a large colourful silk shawl which she draped over her whole head. Again, a timid worrying person is likely to be fearful during his last illness. Such an expectation often proves to be wrong, however. The anxious person may well meet this last stress with greater fortitude than he has shown with his previous chronic burden of doubts and self-questioning.

Among the dying patients I came to know, many of the outward, potentially relevant, aspects of their past and present social life had surprisingly little consistent influence on the likelihood of their being anxious. Their education, their occupational class, their recent financial hardships and so on, might influence the way they described their feelings or the superficial quality of their various apprehensions, but this personal background made little difference to whether they were relatively free of anxiety or not. A window-cleaner, who had left school when thirteen years old, described the same feelings about his likelihood of dying as a university graduate who had become a successful architect; their descriptions of emotions were only unlike in that they used different idioms. There were, however, some aspects of the personal lives of dying people that did seem to have a frequent association with the presence or absence of anxiety. These notably included their religious belief and their ages when they died.

Religious belief is obviously relevant to dying people. It enters the thoughts of so many when they are seriously ill and some seem upheld by their faith. In the patients who were dying in hospital, it was possible to see if the strength of their religious belief and their attendance at church during life influenced their chances of showing anxiety while dying. Although it may be thought that attempts to quantify religious belief and its effects on emotion are out of place, in spite of the crudeness of the assessments the results did appear to make sense. The patients were all nominally Christians, the majority belonging to the Church of England. When asked more directly about their faith, 30 per cent admitted that they had none at all or very little, or they were agnostics. They had acquiesced in being called Christians when others expected them to admit to a religion. They either never went to church or only to partake in social functions which, as far as they were concerned, had only the trappings of religion. About 35 per cent felt that Christianity had a background importance in their lives, but rarely attended church. The remaining third were more sincere Christians, going to church quite frequently. It was only 10 per cent of all these people who were quite firm in their faith and attended services each week. This group of patients did not differ much in their religious beliefs from other larger groups which have been investigated in England.[69]

In what way was their degree of faith associated with their chances of feeling anxious during their last illness? Those who had firm religious faith and attended their church weekly or frequently were most free of anxiety, only a fifth were apprehensive. The next most confident group, in which only a quarter were anxious, were those who had frankly said that they had practically no faith. The tepid believers, who professed faith but made little outward observance of it, were more anxious to a significant extent. They were twice as commonly apprehensive as either the regular church-goers or those without religious faith.[80] What part is played by the

religious belief removing fear and how much is determined by
having a personality more able to adhere to convictions is hard
to say. It was clear that for some people death was made acceptable
in the context of their religious convictions.

The younger people whom I visited in hospital were more
prone to be anxious in their terminal illness. As many as two
thirds of those who died under fifty years of age were clearly
apprehensive, whereas less than a third of those over sixty years
were as anxious. It is understandable that younger people should
be more disquieted by dying. The advent of death at this earlier
stage of life disrupts more expectations and hopes. There was a
more specific association of anxiety and parenthood. Young
mothers and fathers of dependent children showed their under-
standably greater emotional unease. Some of them spoke with
considerable frankness of their apprehension concerning their
children whom they feared they might leave for ever. Perhaps
these younger people were also made more prone to anxiety by
the fact, mentioned in the previous chapter, that they tend to
suffer more physical discomfort in their terminal illness.

DEPRESSION

Although anxiety occurs quite frequently among the dying, it is not
the most common form of emotional distress. Depression is seen
more often; at least, it is if those near to the dying are prepared to
notice it. The sadness and misery that seriously ill people feel in
these circumstances are liable to be underrated by the onlookers
because it is easy to assume that symptoms of depression such as
the loss of interest, incapacity to enjoy things and dulled emotion
are entirely due to the serious physical disease they have. This is
often a wrong assumption; others, who are seriously ill but
expected to recover, do not experience or show the same degree of
misery.[80] If severely ill people are asked, they can usually distinguish their feeling of melancholy from the exhaustion due to
physical illness.

Among the group of dying patients I came to know in the
teaching hospital many spoke of their sadness, and by the time

that they were within two weeks of dying about half were experiencing some depression of mood. The nurses had observed, without necessarily making any close inquiry, that about a quarter of these mortally ill people were quite clearly depressed. The unhappiness that the dying bear can be severe, not just some degree of dejection. Quite a few confessed that they had seriously considered ending their own lives, or they had wished their lives to end because their existence was so miserable. They made such comments as 'I wanted to die at the operation' or 'I wanted to die before coming in [to hospital], but there were no sleeping tablets.' One elderly lady had taken a considerable number of sleeping tablets with the firm intention of killing herself. For some time she had been ill with heart failure and her vision was badly affected by cataracts. At home she looked after a husband who had severe rheumatism. Recently she had been in hospital where a cancer of the bowel had been found and removed, but the operation left her with a colostomy opening at one side of her abdomen. She said that she had never really wanted this operation performed. On her return home she had decided that she would prefer to die and, in fact, still felt that way when her suicidal bid had proved unsuccessful. 'It's all over, it's no use, let me die,' she said. She felt she would never recover and was intensely depressed. She did improve somewhat in her spirits while she was cared for in hospital before death did finally take her.

Suicidal acts are by no means rare events in those who have a serious, perhaps fatal, disease. The limited prospect of the life that remains to them appears miserable, and they anticipate the death they believe their disease is bringing. In a study by Sainsbury of a number of suicides that took place in London, he found that physical illness seemed to be the principal cause for 18 per cent of them killing themselves.[171] In many other cases physical disorders had contributed to their suicide. Most important were the cancers, although often, tragically enough, the post-mortem examination showed apparently successful treatment with no recurrence.

Other investigations of the causes of suicide have confirmed the importance of serious physical illness as a cause.[96, 192] More specifically, one investigation of people in the Bristol area who had killed themselves showed that 4 per cent were suffering from an incurable illness which would probably have ended their lives within six months.[178] Amongst the many troubled people attempting suicide who do not in fact end their own lives, there have been some with a fatal illness.[84] Frequently they have taken an overdose because they despaired of coping any longer and, until the suicidal act, they appeared to get insufficient help.

What causes so many dying people to experience this degree of mental distress and misery, so bad that quite a few consider immediate death preferable? Just the realization that life will shortly come to an end is often accounted a good enough reason for unhappiness, but is certainly not the sole cause, nor does it always bring sadness. Many patients realize that they are dying and have no emotional distress. The illness itself may be the cause if it gives rise to suffering capable of eroding morale. Depression increases as the illness lengthens and if physical discomfort persists.[80] Among the group of patients dying in the teaching hospital, those who were quite free of physical discomfort were rarely markedly depressed. If they had endured much and then treatment brought relief, the unhappiness also tended to go. Steady deterioration, unpleasant exhaustion, increasing discomforts with further symptoms added to those already there, all contributed towards a patient experiencing misery. It is in some ways reassuring that physical discomfort is an important source of mental depression because it is a trouble which can often be alleviated. It also indicates, somewhat accusingly, that in so far as we have not made use of all the suitable methods of relieving physical discomfort or failed to provide enough people and facilities to care adequately for the dying, we have contributed to their misery.

The degree of love and companionship that exists between the dying and those near to them will, of course, influence how they feel. When the mortally ill person looks for affection and does not find it, unhappiness must follow. There is one aspect of human behaviour, saddening but understandable, often observed when a person is known to be dying. This is the avoidance of or emotional withdrawal from those who are about to die.[99] It has been called a 'bereavement of the dying'.[208] The feeling of isolation and grief that this separation can produce in people expecting to die soon must arouse our sympathy. The withdrawal from the dying by those with the prospect of life is understandable, however, for the latter have to cope with the sure anticipation that the person whom they know, and perhaps love, will soon be no more. They already differ in this new, important way, already they share things less. Besides a sadness, they may feel embarrassment because they will live but the sick person is going to die. Sometimes the healthy may even feel a sort of illogical anger at being deserted by the dying, even if the separation is to come through death. The growing emotional separation is revealed to the dying person by the uncertain behaviour of the others, the excluding whispered voices, the hollow cheerfulness, the halting conversations or even the outright avoidance.

This disengagement may, on first consideration, seem universally cruel. Some ill people are very dependent upon the emotional support of others. They may get distressed when no member of the family is within reach. They may live for the visits that loved people make to them in hospital. As one man said: 'If you're going to peg out you might as well just get on with it. But it's better when my son or someone comes of an evening.' If such emotional bonds are threatened by the spiritual withdrawal of others, it does unkindly bring misery. It is not always one-sided, however. Although some dying people make it obvious how much they depend upon personal contact, others begin to withdraw into an emotional isolation. It may be that the dying may find parting too painful and, as in ordinary life, they wish to avoid the atmosphere of good-byes which anticipates separation. One dying man told me of all the arrangements he had made to safeguard the future of his wife and daughter whom he loved, but he almost dreaded his wife's visits because they made him so upset. Others retreat a little more gradually into themselves without any feeling that they are avoiding sorrow – things just do not matter so much any longer.

Besides the unhappiness from physical discomfort and the sense of separation that illness can bring, there is sorrow at losing some of the positive attributes of living. While they lie dying, patients feel the loss of health and strength and then the loss of the familiar role they have been accustomed to play. It is painful for people to recognize that they will no longer be, say, an effective mother to the children or that they have become a liability instead of the provider to the family. The dying begin to lose their sense of belonging, and losses bring grief. Death, which they face, threatens to take away everyone and everything valued in life. Is it not natural to grieve in preparation for the losses to come? This sorrow may not easily go into words although it can be tacitly shared.[106]

The manner of people's previous adjustment to life is bound to influence the way they view its end. Death can be very distressing if viewed as the final disillusionment, and this can well occur in those who have seen their lives as a sequence of blighted hopes. If a person has always been self-doubting or guilt-laden, the coming of death and its taking away all remaining hopes of expiation during life can cause profound depression. Among the observations of dying patients made by a psychiatrist, Cappon, he describes how he found out that a patient's distress when facing death grew out of his manner of coping with life.[32] A person may manage to present a stable front to the world throughout his lifetime only by a series of complex psychological manoeuvres. These ways of compensating for inward strife, these defences of the ego, are also likely to determine the sort of response made to approaching death. Sometimes the prospect of death is so overwhelming that the usual methods of coping with an emotionally disturbing situation break down. If a dying person can no longer use effectively his usual psychological tricks that prevent too outrageous uncertainty, if defensive tactics such as denying the unpleasant or blaming others are no longer effective, then he may experience distress to the full.

The unhappiness of the dying can acquire a bitter flavour for a number of reasons. Sorrow will be tinged with resentment if it seems unjust for them to be dying now. This sense of injustice is usually greater in those who had expected a longer life, who had planned for greater success or enjoyment in their later years. Even though this may have been but fantasy, they may feel that death's coming has robbed them of this anticipated life's goal while some

undeserving people unfairly enjoy long lives. When aggrieved by
the prospect of dying before they had expected to, fatally ill
patients may become jealous of those around them who retain
their health, becoming irritable with those whose strength seems
to mock them.

Another source of bitterness arises in those who cannot surrender to their growing weakness. Frequently their lives have been
noteworthy for self-control and orderliness. When dying, they
resent the loss of control over their fate and the sense of adequacy
they have always striven for in life. They are angry with their own
failing bodies and they are also apt to criticize and blame others.
Those who care for the dying know what a problem such people
are to themselves and others. One such aggrieved patient in
hospital greatly troubled the nurses and doctors who cared for her;
they were torn by pity mixed with irritation and devotion marred
by a sense of failure. Often young nurses would leave her bedside
to shed a few tears in a quiet spot, if they could find one, because
their attempts to help her had been met by contemptuous dis-
missal. Occasionally she would refuse treatment altogether or
criticize a nurse's particular clumsiness or ineptitude. It was not
that she was a continuously nagging person against whom one
could steel one's heart. She could often show herself to be the
warm-hearted, somewhat opinionated charlady that she had
formerly been; she could speak of her own feelings and her im-
potence against the cancer that was killing her and she apologized
for the trouble she caused. But soon she would again lash with her
tongue, criticizing her doctor for not making the diagnosis early
enough, and accusing those who were treating her of apathy,
inefficiency and callousness. She had always wanted to achieve
more than being a cleaner and, although ill-educated, was intelligent enough. It was a way of expressing her disappointment
and bitterness she had for herself and the life that seemed unfulfilled.

Another bitter pang of depression can come when the dying feel
that after their own death, those who are left behind may manage
too well without them. The need to belong is of profound importance to people. Some are possessive and require the bonds of

friendship to be constantly demonstrated, if they are not to feel insecure. A dying patient's suspicion that a companion could manage very well after his own death, can bring gall into what is left of their partnership. The dying person who feels that his passing will be little mourned, has a hurt to his pride and may also sense a greater annihilation in his approaching death. It is just as well for the dying, and for those who care for them, that when resentment of those who are going to live does arise, it usually gives way to softer feelings. If it is sustained, it may destroy potential sympathy. In their terminal illness people often have a great need for the emotional support and understanding of others – even if they do occasionally test the strength of the bond – because there are so many dark patches in their changing pattern of feelings.

DOES EMOTIONAL ANGUISH HASTEN DEATH?

In the close association of dying and mental distress, it is often suggested that the emotions of man can bring about his own death. It is quite possible that emotions are one of the many contributing causes which together influence the rate of progress towards death, but this does not mean that emotions are often the final arbiter of death through some mystical process. It may well be that troubled feelings disorder a physiological process in a way which loosens a tennous hold on life. Albeit there are many anecdotes of dramatic deaths which have occurred at times of emotional crisis or have been inspired by magical beliefs.[31, 77] Tales are told of voodoo deaths visited upon the believing victim, stories of mock executions that have ended in death from panic. These accounts are not often first hand and tend to grow in dramatic value as they are handed on.

There are well authenticated instances, however, of sudden death consequent upon an abrupt shock. These tragedies are probably due to the heart stopping from a catastrophic over-action of the autonomic nervous system. Whether the emotional aspect of shock plays a causal role in such events, or the vital sequence is mediated through nervous reflexes with or without some parallel emotion, is hard to say. A death of this sort, induced by sudden stress, has been studied in captured wild rats by Richter.[159] By subjecting these most untame creatures to being handled by man, having their whiskers trimmed and being made to swim, they uniformly die. The procedures, although presumably unpleasant for the animal, do not have fatal results for tame rats or wild rats which have become more accustomed to handling. The death of the wild rat in these circumstances, which would appear to produce emotional strain, seems to be due to changes in the impulses along the vagus nerve to the heart, so that it slows and then ceases to beat. The analogous sudden deaths in man usually occur with painful or dramatic bodily sensations, such as abrupt immersion in water or some minor surgical procedure in a conscious patient. A psycho-logical stress can apparently precipitate death in patients in a precarious state of health. For example, sudden deaths with little or no warning sometimes happen when patients are apparently on the road to recovery following a coronary thrombosis. It has been found that such deaths in hospital are more likely to happen during the formal ward rounds of the physician visiting his patients, especially if a patient is keyed up, anticipating some authoritative pronouncement on his case.[95]

Besides these sudden deaths occurring in a setting of emotional stress, there are the less swift deaths which are reported, usually in primitive societies, when a person, believing himself to be fatally bewitched, withdraws in spiritual anguish and dies. We have little of the relevant information to decide what process mediates death through witchcraft. It usually occurs in circumstances where there is no trained scientific observer with facilities to note the bodily changes of the victim – were he present, the circumstances might be inimical to successful magic. It is most probable that in many cases the victim neglects to eat, drink or care for himself. Many people in our culture who develop a severe depressive illness would die were it not for the fact that they are treated and receive care for their neglected bodily needs as well as their state of mind.

There is tragically enough, information available from the situations of great adversity when thousands of prisoners died in camps during the 1939–45 war. The emotional balance of Jewish prisoners in concentration camps directly affected their chances of survival. Tas reported from Bergen-Belsen that depressive symptoms could soon end in death.[194] Of a group of three thousand Jewish prisoners, 70 per cent died in a year in the harsh circumstances of exhaustion, starvation, forced labour, dysentery and so on. As soon as they became apathetic with depression and gave up the continuous struggle to eat and care for themselves, they died. If a doctor could relieve their depression with psychotherapy, the effect was demonstrably life-saving.

American prisoners of war in Japanese hands had a parallel experience. Nardini has painted the grim circumstances of thirty thousand men, only 40 per cent of whom survived their three years imprisonment.[139] Most of them experienced periods of apathy and depression when it was difficult to summon the will to continue the struggle for survival. The determination to survive was normally bolstered by their ignoring some hardships, resorting to fantasy, retaining a sense of some individuality, and directing humour and surreptitious acts against the captors. By these means the courageous were better able to resist not only the sense of defeat, but illness and death.

These conditions demonstrating the interplay of emotional distress and the surrender of life are rather extreme examples to apply to the more normal ending of life in home or hospital. They do point, however, to the part which may be played by the resistance or submission to death in those with fatal illness. The courage of the prisoner hoping to survive his ordeal has its parallels with the patient facing a fatal illness. The ill person has his moments of belief that he will overcome all adversity and his moments when he feels like surrendering. Often a point is reached when the mortally ill person appears to acquiesce in a more rapid progress to death. It may be that some further deterioration of his bodily health has taken place and he is aware that this must be death coming. The onlooker senses that there is no more struggle, and, if it has been a difficult period of suffering, often observes the change with thankfulness. The dying person then appears to be in little distress or none at all. It seems to become a fitting and an inevitable progress towards the end of mortal life. Many have this calm acceptance for some while before they die, but not all do.

8   Awareness and Denial: Struggle and Acceptance

In order to appreciate the attitude of the dying to their situation, it is necessary to have, first of all, some idea of what they know about their state. Are they usually aware that they are dying?

AWARENESS

There is considerable controversy over the extent of the awareness that the dying have about their approaching end. One distinguished physician wrote:

As for the dying man himself, we rarely find him 'looking death in the face' and knowing it is death. He is either very dubious that death is coming to him, or his apperception is so dimmed, whether by weakness or by a merciful physician, that the end of life is a dream-state rather than a true awareness.[85]

In contrast, another doctor has written:

Most dying patient have the feeling that death is near. Some know it well enough and yet want nothing said about it: or perhaps, while they like to talk of it with the doctors and nurses, they cannot bear to speak of it to their families.[214]

These two views have been selected, not only as they illustrate the divergence of opinion but also because they have been expressed by two thoughtful, experienced physicians, whose opinions should not be readily dismissed.

Why is it that some who care for the dying are sure that few realize that they are dying, while others are convinced that most dying people are quite aware of what is happening to them? First, it depends on the opportunities given to patients to feel free to talk about such things. Given the chance, many more reveal what they suspect or know. Opportunities depend not only upon time but upon the attitude of the listener. Some doctors consciously or unconsciously do not wish their patients to speak of their death which they, as doctors, are failing to prevent. The patient may appreciate this lack of receptiveness and keep silent to avoid embarrassment.

A second reason for divergent views is that different doctors may work with different groups of patients who may not have the same chances of learning that their illness is likely to be fatal. Patients whose last illness is treated by their usual doctor in outwardly similar fashion to their previous illnesses may have little reason to think their present illness is fatal, especially if their doctor is a reticent man. Patients with conditions requiring special treatment in hospital, such as radiotherapy in a hospital for the treatment of cancer, do have reason to suspect that their illness is a threat to life. Of course, with some patients death comes so swiftly that they have little time to be aware that they are dying.

A third reason for uncertainty is the difficulty of being sure what dying people really do believe about their condition. It is possible to be left in doubt even after fatally ill people have spoken of their views on the outcome of their illness, since very likely they themselves are quite uncertain. Can we say that they are aware of dying if they voice an occasional suspicion, or if they express a fear that they might die, or even if they speak of conscious fantasies of future life which they seem to realize are but day-dreams? Moreover dying people are apt to speak or hint sombrely of the outlook at one time and talk lightly of hopeful plans soon after. Sometimes the hints that they give are fairly clear indications that they are aware of being near death. Glances are exchanged and the tone of voice, or the manner of referring to things in life, all go towards establishing a mutual intuitive understanding between patients and those who care for them. Sometimes spontaneous disclaimers of anxiety or deliberate avoidance of reference to the future, except in the vaguest terms, show that the outcome is suspected. This intuitive sympathy is of great personal value, but it is not incontrovertible evidence of people's awareness of dying. Therefore it is possible for others to feel that the dying are aware or unaware according to their own views on the matter.

Only a few people now assert that no one ever realizes that they are dying. Two of the studies of dying patients that include an assessment of their awareness have said that about a quarter of the patients were aware of the final outcome. One of these reports was based on a study of over two hundred patients who died in a geriatric unit.[51] Their awareness was judged by their remarks and by their attitude to relatives and nurses. Exton-Smith, who made the study, said that this assessment of one quarter knowing might be an underestimate. Time was insufficient in a busy hospital ward to get to know patients really well and many more may have suspected a fatal outcome without spontaneously revealing it. The other report concerned the care of patients with terminal cancer at home. The general practitioners reported that although only 11 per cent definitely knew their condition, up to 25 per cent had a good idea of the truth.[211]

Two further studies of dying people have included assessments of whether they are aware of dying. When Elisabeth Kubler-Ross interviewed fatally ill patients in a Chicago hospital and asked them to talk of their experience, she reported that only three out of two hundred patients attempted to deny death's approach right to the last[106]. This did not mean that the dying would not often demonstrate their hopes of recovery. Cartwright and Anderson's broader survey in Britain noted that according to the informants seen not long after the person had died, more than half of the patients knew what was wrong with them.[36] It also appeared that very nearly a half probably or definitely knew that they were unlikely to recover.

It is the opinion of Cicely Saunders that many people do come to know that they are dying. She has had wide experience as nurse, almoner and now as doctor treating people with chronic or with terminal illness in a hospital devoted to their care.

She has said:

In my own experience I find that the truth dawns gradually on many, even most, of the dying even when they do not ask and are not told. They accept it quietly and often gratefully but some may not wish to discuss it and we must respect their reticence.[173]

My own observations of the patients in a general hospital have led me to the same conclusion.

During my first bedside visit to each of these patients who were to die I took note of the comments they made regarding the outcome. Quite a number, 38 per cent, did not speak of their future outlook at all or used only vague terms. They made use of such non-committal remarks as 'I must take it steady', or spoke more of their hopes than their prognoses – 'I was hoping to be better by now' or 'I'm determined to get on'. Only 5 per cent seemed confident of recovery, for example a man whose cancer had been confirmed on recent operation said with conviction 'I shall win through'; more commonly such phrases are only buoys to hopes. A further 8 per cent anticipated partial recovery.

The other 49 per cent of the dying patients soon showed that they were neither ignorant nor evasive of the fact that their illness might be fatal. Quite a few, 18 per cent, spoke of it as a possibility. It was put very succinctly by a quietly courageous man who knew he had cancer, 'I can't think about the future, but I know my family is well provided for.' Many of the patients, 26 per cent, were more sure than this, saying firmly, for instance, 'I don't think I'm going to get better.' A tough, independent window-cleaner rapidly worsening with a malignant illness affecting his nervous system said of his condition, 'I hope I'll get better – I've only just come in [to hospital]. But if I don't – well – I'll just go off home after six or seven weeks. Better finish off there.' A few, 6 per cent, were unhesitating about their approaching death. The calm statement 'I'm going to die' became familiar but never unimpressive. In summary, it can be stated that half of these people dying in hospital, even at the first interview, took the opportunity to talk frankly and spoke of the possibility or certainty that they were to die soon.

I continued to visit these people in hospital every week. We conversed at length or briefly, depending upon their inclination or strength; many of them said they were pleased at the chance to talk so freely. Often we came to know each other well – friendships grew fast in these circumstances and sometimes it seemed difficult to believe we met only a few times. By the end of their lives the majority had spoken of the possibility of dying. A few wished to speak of it several times, but it was not a matter which they all wished to discuss frequently; sometimes it was voiced briefly once or perhaps fully discussed and then not mentioned again. Mutual understanding was tacit thenceforward. When they did speak of the possibility of death they often said that recognition had been there for some little while but they had not admitted it before. Occasionally if there was a temporary improvement in their physical well-being or a lifting of mood as discomfort was relieved, they started to believe in recovery. Considered as a group, however, those patients who remained and died in the hospital came to know more and more certainly that death was approaching. In fact, only a quarter of these patients did not speak spontaneously to me at some time of their awareness that death might come soon, and at least a fifth became quite certain that they were dying. Although I had formerly thought that at least some people knew when they were dying, the actual frequency of awareness surprised me then, though my subsequent experience has confirmed it.

It was not possible to be sure how these people came to realize that they were dying. Not many had been clearly told that they had diseases, such as a tumour, which they would know could prove fatal. Very few, if any, had heard their doctors use the word cancer, because this word now has in the lay mind even more sinister implications than it warrants. None of them apparently had been told outright by a doctor that they might be dying – although it had sometimes been referred to by their priest. In general, the particular type of illness or particular symptom that these hospital patients had, did not have any consistent influence on their awareness. If severe illness persisted for months, or if discomfort continued in spite of treatment, then they spoke more often of the chances of a fatal outcome.

With one exception, it did not seem that any particular aspect of personal life or background was consistently likely to make a person realize that he might be dying. The exception was that those with young children, sadly enough, were more likely to talk of the fact that they might be dying. Religious views, age, educational or occupational background had no predictable effect in fostering people's awareness. It was possible to underestimate initially the awareness of people who were not used to being articulate about personal feelings, and one could be slower to gain understanding of the less well educated if they felt hesitant at talking freely with the professional people in the hospital world. Their awareness was no different, however. For instance a so-called general dealer who made a living from discarded household goods was slowly dying in hospital from cancer. All the staff thought he had no appreciation of his condition, he never said much about his health except occasionally to ask for a good tonic. Indeed he seemed to meet each event of the day with no more than some well-worn phrase or cliché in a Cockney voice. Once, as I sat by his bed and he carried on the conversation by reading and commenting on the various dramatic and tragic events in his newspaper, he interpolated a revealing comment on his recent departure from home to re-enter hospital,

The wife was upset, as she's never seen me like it. So I said we've all got to go, girl. I've had a good life – it doesn't worry me. Now those two honeymoon couples killed on the front page. They're the ones I'm sorry for. Not me. I'm all right.

He digressed on to the next column dealing with news of old-age pensions.

Awareness of dying seems to grow from a number of clues. When no improvement lasts, when further symptoms are added to those already present and when there are obvious signs that the body is not functioning properly, these signals plus a sense of overwhelming exhaustion warn patients that they have no ordinary illness. It is not all that rare for patients to find out about their illness by getting or making an opportunity to read the hospital notes about themselves. Other clues come from overheard snatches of conversation by hospital staff about their incurable condition. Occasionally doctors at the bedside show gross forgetfulness or lack of consideration; intent on discussing the illness, they may forget the patient. More often the hints are gathered by alert patients gleaning all the little implications in the demeanour of nurses and doctors, such as the facial expression of a doctor contemplating clinical evidence which shows him that he cannot cure, the rather abrupt injunction to the patient 'not to worry', given without further explanation, or the kindly reassurance which either does not ring true or is spoken in obituary tones. Visitors and relatives who have been warned that a person will not recover may be unable to stop their own emotions from betraying their knowledge to the patient. This is especially so if a number of relatives, who have been out of touch for a long time, pay an unexpected visit and seem ill at ease. For those ill people who wish to draw conclusions about their chances of recovery, the signs are usually there.

DENIAL

But not everyone wants to know. Some never admit to themselves or anyone else that they are dying. A few assert that all will be well, with remarks like 'I'll be all right', 'I shall win through'. Perhaps they may have no reason to think otherwise, but often their words imply that they are unwilling to consider the possibility of dying. They may well be quite unaware of this protective function of their own mind which subconsciously deviates from thoughts of fatal illness. Some people tend throughout life to ignore or deny unpleasant possibilities which threaten their equanimity. During their terminal illness this evasion continues; even if they are aware that others believe them to be dying, they have a firm belief that they will live and the others will be proved wrong.[142]

If thoroughly successful in deceiving themselves, such patients may present a picture of bland cheerfulness. Often the attempt to deny to themselves the possibility of their illness proving fatal is only partially successful, an inadequate buttress against fear. Sometimes the shifting from blind hope to recurring anxiety seems to make things worse, as occurred in a man in his sixties who was reaching the end of a long chronic fatal disease of lymph glands. He often asserted that he was 'getting on all right, now', although it was patently clear to all that this was not so. When he made remarks like, 'I'm not going to worry any more. That's finished now', and yet looked very agitated it was apparent how unsuccessfully he was trying to fend off his misgivings. Nevertheless, quite a few benefit from a protective evasion of the terrible thought of dying, although fairly conscious of the fact that it is only a false denial. They feel that they are better off if they never consider their fate in stark clarity. They use such comments as 'I look on the bright side of things' or 'I don't think about the future'. On the whole such people rely less on repeated ill-founded protestations of improvement and more on the avoidance of talking and thinking about the matter.

A very adequate realization of the true state of affairs is no bar to the use of denial. Even those who had spoken in definite terms of their awareness of dying, quite often took refuge in some unemphatic disclaimer of the true outlook. Few wish to hold constantly in mind the thought that death is coming very close. After all, if it is not absolutely certain that they are dying, there is no reason why grim foreboding should not be softened by some comforting inconsistency. A woman who once or twice spoke of the inexorable progress of her fatal cancer, often chatted lightly about life and the future as if she had only some passing ailment. Mental ease demands that the waking thoughts of the dying should often be concerned with the trivia of the moment and pleasant memories. If thoughts do turn to the future, there is pleasure in toying with light hopes and fantasies. There is no reason why the dying should not have the comfort of make-believe and even invite those around them to share these consoling day-dreams and not shatter them. At times they can again show full insight or give a hint to companions that they are well aware that it is a game, an acceptable façade. The convention of not talking directly about dying can often be a useful comfort to fall back upon.[156]

STRUGGLE

Some unfortunate people combine an awareness that they may be dying with an extreme reluctance to do so. As long as they are unable to surrender to their inevitable progress to the end, they are liable to be in distress. About a quarter of those I visited in the teaching hospital showed this sort of struggle and others may well have had similar distress at some time during their last illness. Kübler-Ross considers that the normal pattern of adjustment to dying involves a period of denial and then a phase of anger, rage, envy and resentment.[106] Many who care for the dying have indelible memories of people who have had this mental anguish, as like as not of a young person, who feared to be torn from life. Such distress is commoner in younger adults, especially those with small children, although, of course, such acute regret and fear is by no means confined to the young.

When the dying have such a fearful reluctance to go, all those near to them are involved in the distress.[65] If this occurs in a hospital, the nurses are troubled in spirit, perhaps tearful or taking refuge in too professional a calm. The doctors, who are to some extent shielded from immediate or frequent contact with the patient, find themselves attempting to resolve an insoluble problem and, owing to their own disquiet, do not always make best use of their judgement. All are apt to be entangled in discontent with themselves and with the others. It happened in the case of an attractive woman of twenty-five who had been increasingly ill over two years with a fatal gland disorder. She had not been married very long and had one young child. She had improved several times, each improvement being a little less marked, a little shorter, than the last. Then she re-entered hospital for what was clearly going to be the last time. She was terribly frightened, often clutching hold of people she knew and entreating them to get her better again. She kept asking to be reassured that she was beginning to recover, and sometimes quietened a little if she was told that she would be better again. But reassurance in these circumstances does not help for long; the dying person who so strongly suspects the truth cannot wholly believe statements about

getting better. When there is worsening health and repeated unrewarding alterations in treatment, all of which are explained away
somewhat differently by nurses, doctors, relatives, hospital
orderlies or other patients, how can there be confidence in recovery, however much it is desired? This poor girl was repeatedly
given reassurances, which was in accordance with the policy of the
consultant in charge of her who had decided she could not face a
more honest opinion; but yet her distress continued. Finally, the
chaplain answered her questions with greater honesty. Although
she was very unhappy to know more certainly that she was dying,
her terror and conflict abated considerably.

A few dying people fear death and try to fight it or escape it
right to the end. Dissatisfied with their doctors, who are not curing
them, they accept treatment only from those who promise to cure.
They are tempted to go from one doctor to another, or to turn to
other healers, including the misguided and the charlatans who
make confident but quite unjustified claims. Most patients remain
with the same doctor but they may demand or implore that he do
more. They may even refuse treatments which can do no more than
relieve discomfort, and abhor drugs that threaten to take away their
mental alertness because they feel those drugs may enforce their
unwilling surrender. If their extreme reluctance to die does not
evolve into acceptance, peace may not come until the very end.

Although the onlooker may find it heart-rending to witness the
hopeless struggle of the one who fears to die, it may not necessarily
be the worst way for the patient to face his end. Admittedly it is
hard to find much comfort in the situation of the dying man who
says outright 'I don't want to die' and continues a doomed struggle
against incurable illness, but he may well need the hope and the
refusal to surrender. Even the unavailing struggle may be preferable to the desolation of no hope at all.

Although those who suspect that they have a fatal illness may
eventually find ease in surrendering to death, many are long kept
from reaching this calm because they do not know how far they
are from death. This was touched on in a very factual way by one
middle-aged man a month before he finally did die – he had neared
death several times in the last six months but had occasionally been

well enough to return to work for a short time. Sometimes he wanted to give up making any more effort: 'If I knew I was going to peg out in ten months, I would just want to put my feet up.' Those who move steadily towards the end in some ways have an easier time than those who have greater uncertainty in a potentially fatal illness. In poor health, the latter know that although a sudden fatal crisis – another stroke, another heart attack – could occur at any moment, it might perhaps not take place for a long time, even perhaps that there will be no crisis, only an irregular deterioration. People with such illnesses, especially if they lead a restricted hospital life, are apt to feel resentful. They know the disease will be with them until they die, but they are not really dying. They fear that efforts on their part to do more and defy the illness may precipitate a crisis in their health. They may also feel that the medical staff around them do not expect nor wholeheartedly work for their cure, but at the same time imply that they, the patients, do not make enough effort to help themselves.[38] Many are glad when at last they can give up the struggle to live against such odds.

ACCEPTANCE

In the fatally ill, acceptance and resignation to death seem appropriate, permitting peace of mind. When dying is inevitable, submission in the struggle for life is no personal failure, because greater determination will not prevent death. Many patients become almost indifferent to their leaving life, even though fully conscious. They may be less troubled than the onlookers.[104] Glaser and Strauss have studied the complex interaction of patients, family and hospital staff as each of them come to what terms they can with the fact that the patient is going to die.[66] Given time, acceptance usually comes, but not necessarily to all the characters on the stage. With irregular pace there is an evolution, often through a troubled period of doubt and emotional turbulence, to a more peaceful, possibly sad, surrender.

The progress towards acceptance may sometimes appear simple but is often uneven and wayward. To read the published diary of Diana Gault who struggled and coped courageously with

three years of progressive illness until her death in 1967 can give
an insight into the hope, the despair, the humour, the suffering,
the happiness and the sadness of an individual travelling towards
final acceptance along what she called her journey.[60]

Life's happenings and the course of a disease can twist and
turn the path through the fatal illness as in the case of a pleasant
labouring man who had a cancer of the lung. The disease had
been discovered only a short while after his wife had been killed
in a road accident. At that time he was not sure if he wanted to
live much longer or not, but after an operation for his cancer,
he regained physical and moral strength and said quite spontaneously that now he wanted to go on living. Unfortunately
all the lung cancer could not be removed and some months later
he returned to hospital because the disease had caused his swallowing to become difficult. Another small palliative operation helped
him for a while and he expressed confidence in the treatment he
had received when he left hospital. Once again he fell ill and now
expressed both hopes and doubts about his outlook. 'I don't think
my breathing will ever get better,' he said. A week later he was
worse and confessed, 'You just don't know what's going to
happen.' On the day he died he told the ward sister that he was now
aware that he was dying. He did not want to be bothered with the
oxygen any more and asked if she could stay with him a moment.
He held on to her hand as she sat beside him while he lost consciousness and died shortly after.

About one person in four dying in a general hospital showed this
degree of acceptance and positive composure.[82] Different circumstances might easily alter the overall picture, of course, but in
the absence of other information these hospital patients have been
used as a guide. Many speak quite positively of this feeling of
consenting to life's ending, often they use the word *accept*, saying
that they have had a good life. It is equally common for the dying to
reveal an attitude of slightly less positive acceptance of approaching death, but without distress. They acknowledge what is happening without further comment or perhaps refer to it with only a little
regret. Although well aware that they may be dying, they may not
wish to relinquish all hope of recovery. If we include those few

patients who become impatient for death because their remaining
life is so unrewarding or distressing, it seems that at least half of the
dying come both to acknowledge openly and to accept the nearing
end to their life. Such acceptance is more common in the elderly.
Another quarter speak with distress of their possible death and the
other quarter say little about it. The few, just mentioned, who are
impatient for death raise great problems, which will be discussed
in Chapter 11. Acceptance has lost its positive value for peace if
the dying are forced to say 'It has gone on too long' or 'Let me die'.

Acceptance of death can come quickly. Many who die quite
suddenly can have time to realize that this is their probable fate but
little time to feel emotional distress. Awareness and enforced
acceptance may come together. This is inferred from accounts of
those who have been near to death. Some wartime recollections of
dramatic escapes from death showed that the accompanying
thoughts could be almost banal, such as 'This is the end of everything', and the matter-of-fact thoughts of a man in a crashing air-
craft: 'This'll be another,' he murmured to himself and wondered
who would write to his home.[145] A classic personal account of a
fall, very likely to have been fatal, was given by Albert Heim, a
mountaineer. During the five or ten seconds of his fall he saw his
possible fate, the results for those left behind, and saw countless
pictures of his past life. It was all without pain or fear or anguish,
he said, peaceful and tranquil until his fall was ended with a thud
that he heard.[75]

Those who arrive at a slower, more peaceful acceptance of
mortal illness require more than momentary resolution. Some
stoical people have a resolute calm which is either an innate
attribute or the product of years of successful emotional schooling.
Many accept their own death according to the philosophy of life
and death that they had formerly held, although their often ill-
formulated philosophy may require revision when the problem
has become more immediate and personal. They may make a
spiritual and perhaps some practical preparations to depart this
life. Thoughts turn towards the continuation of life after death.
It may be to an orthodox religious belief, or some personal
conviction that they are about to rejoin loved people who have

died previously. They may have thoughts of the threads of continuing life in this world, with interest focused on children and grandchildren who are a promise of future continuation. They can deny their total annihilation in this world or the next by clear statements of faith or by less direct remarks. 'I've seen my grandson and now I'm satisfied,' said one woman who only a few days before had been fearful of dying. Another lady who spoke of her regret at parting from her husband became reconciled to it a few days before dying with the thought that she was joining her mother who had died a little while ago.

Making the practical preparations for their approaching death can be an important and sometimes an emotionally rewarding task for the dying. They wish to leave no unfinished problems for their families. They complete the major tasks, like winding up their business affairs and making sure their will is in order. They often take great care over the minor arrangements – where they have put things and who is to have the small personal properties – so that there should be no subsequent disagreements. Often the dying take pleasure in knowing that all is handed over in good order to their successors. It was pleasant to see the satisfaction of one seventy-year-old man near to death after he had signed the final letter to his bank. He visibly relaxed, saying, 'It's all settled now.' These actions can similarly comfort those aware that they might die, but unsure if it is inevitable. One man said:

I thought my life would be cut short but I have great confidence in what the hospital can do for me. I have a tumour. My wife and the firm know and provisions have been made for the future.

Those who wholly accept their dying are not always concerned with weighty thoughts and the consequences of their mortal illness. They even show a quiet enjoyment of their relaxation, now that the struggles of life are over. Not infrequently, being seriously ill and concentration beginning to cloud, they regard events in a very drowsy fashion. If they are alert, they may be quite content to let their minds play on the happenings of the moment, the little events of the day. In what order shall they take their now unimportant medicines? What little bits of news will their visitors bring? How attentive that nurse is and how nice she looks! And thoughts wander pleasantly where they will.

Many dying show their kindness and become, perhaps, more noble in spirit than they have ever been. They do all they can to spare the feelings of those they are going to leave behind to bear their loss. Before relatives visit, they prepare their appearance and compose their faces so that those who love them should not believe they suffer. They demonstrate their affection in both apparent and in subtle ways. These are the people who often take great care of the feelings of their nurses and doctors. In candid moments, when they know it is possible to speak freely without embarrassment, these generous souls may tell how they help those around them. They may say how they have avoided the unkindness of putting certain frank questions to a doctor who, they felt, could never bring himself to tell them that they were dying and would be forced into lies or half-truths that they would recognize. These ill people will also intuitively or consciously avoid any comments or questions that could possibly be construed by others to indicate anything but gratitude for their help and faith in their ability. Sometimes patients can accept better than a doctor that they can still have undiminished trust in his care, although he is quite unable to cure them. They can often accept more completely than those around them that they are about to die.

Given sufficient spiritual and bodily help, it is probable that most of those moving steadily towards death would experience the peace of surrendering to their fate before they drift into permanent unconsciousness. Many do attain this calm acceptance, some do not. Some, unfortunately, wish for death because they suffer. We must consider the treatment that is required to make the dying sufficiently comforted for them to reach a quiet acceptance of death.

Care of the Dying

9   Treatment for the Dying

The physical and emotional discomfort that the dying are liable to suffer are implicit indications of the care that they require. Some of these needs are automatically recognized and met. It is only when the neglected patient is seen that one realizes how much of civilized care is taken for granted. A great deal is done to help the dying; so much, in fact, with so many variations according to individual requirements, that it is not feasible to attempt to condense all of the available knowledge, ideas and aims into a single chapter. Some aspects of physical and emotional care will be considered, bearing in mind especially the great importance that personal feelings have in the treatment of incurably ill people. The emphasis must always lie upon tending the person, not battling with his disease, treating the one who feels symptoms, not just treating the symptoms.

THE RELIEF OF PHYSICAL DISCOMFORT

Drugs are not the only means of easing people's suffering. Other methods of treating incurable illness may be very effective in eradicating the more troublesome symptoms of the disease, even if these measures do not necessarily prolong life. Surgery may help a great deal, even when it does not cure. Obstructions of the bowel, which bring pain, can be by-passed by safe standardized operations. Painful cancers may be removed surgically even when it is apparent that all the tumour cannot be taken away. Radiotherapy may eliminate or prevent the distressing symptoms of incurable conditions. For example, if a lung tumour obstructs or threatens to obstruct breathing, irradiation may well destroy this local growth and relieve the feeling of suffocation. The patient may die later of other effects of the tumour, but he will have had more days of relative health and perhaps an easier death. Various medicinal agents may halt the progress of cancers, relieving for a long while, perhaps, pain from growths in bone. The weakness and breathlessness of leukaemia and similar blood diseases can be countered for a while, often years, by measures which delay the development of the abnormal blood cells, while transfusions make good the blood deficiency. Used appropriately, these and many other palliative treatments are immensely valuable.

For some patients such palliative measures either have no part to play, or there comes a time when they have little further to offer. If the dying in these circumstances have discomfort, relief is sought through treatments which prevent the discomfort from being felt. The most notorious discomfort is pain and this possibility often concerns people much more than the fact that they are going to die. Very often pain is entirely relieved. If there were a sufficient number of trained people prepared and able to devote adequate time to give full attention to dying patients in pain, even less suffering would occur. Many doctors interested in the problem have shown what can be achieved.

Pain can be relieved directly by drugs that dull its perception and by measures that interrupt the conduction of pain from diseased parts of the body to the brain. With mild pain the treatment is usually very simple. Analgesic drugs like aspirin, codeine and so on are very effective and they have brought untold relief to millions. Quite a few incurable diseases are liable, in the later stages, to give rise to a more severe pain which is not sufficiently relieved by the commoner analgesics. Many new pain-relieving drugs are produced and a few prove to have some advantage over their predecessors. This book is no place to debate in detail the choice and use of the most effective drugs for relieving pain or any other symptom. Such information can be found in various medical and pharmacological writings. Most doctors have their favourite selection of drugs and get to know how to use them to their best advantage.

For pain, if it persists, sooner or later doctors will turn to the drugs derived from opium, usually morphine or heroin. There is normally a reluctance to prescribe these drugs because, although they have no equal in controlling pain, they are drugs of addiction. Increasing doses are needed to bring about the necessary effect. They are drugs having a marked psychological action, allaying fear and bringing calm and even an unnatural ecstasy. It is not surprising that morphine is so effective in relieving pain if one remembers that this distressing symptom of being in pain is compounded of the perception of painful sensations and the accompanying emotional discomfort. Indeed, the authoritative opinion of one pharmacologist is that these analgesics exert their principal action not on the 'original pain' but on the 'psychological processing' of pain.[17] The increasing tolerance of large doses of morphia or heroin and the increasing need of the patient for the drugs, characteristic of addiction, should rarely be a bar to their use for the dying. Knowing that opiates are drugs of addiction, however, does make it difficult for those caring for the dying to judge if the time has come to use morphia, especially if the illness is chronic and death a long way off. If anything, it seems that there is too much error on the side of caution. In patients with chronic, severe pain regular and adequate doses of morphine or heroin can both relieve the existing pain and prevent it building up again. Then the patient is confident that the pain is controllable, and a need for increasing doses or an undue dependence of the patient on the drug do not often constitute a great problem in the dying.[176]

Another approach to the relief of pain is to interrupt the passage of pain impulses from the diseased area to the relevant parts of the brain concerned in the appreciation of pain. The nerve fibres can be temporarily anaesthetized or more permanently damaged by injecting chemical agents; they can also be cut. This will leave the area supplied by the nerve numb, but free from pain. If this treatment is restricted to suitable cases, it is effective enough. Only too often, unfortunately, the pain is not limited to an area which has just one or two convenient sensory nerves easily interrupted. Sometimes relief can come from cutting the tracts of fibres carrying pain sensation along the spinal cord, although it is no easy thing to sever just the right fibres and no more. The other possible places to interfere with the appreciation of pain are in certain parts of the brain, frequently the thalamus and the frontal lobe.[154] In a proportion of people distressed by continuous pain, operations in these areas have been of great help in either removing the pain sensation or the distress which accompanies the pain. It can be quite strange talking to a person who, following the operation of leucotomy, will, if anyone asks, describe the pain he can still feel, but as a sensation which no longer gives rise to distress. It is the sort of disturbing change of a person's reactions that one hesitates to bring about except for the fact that his prior state had already been so sadly changed by pain and intolerable distress.

Pain can be relieved more easily and effectively than many other physical discomforts which trouble dying people. For some of these discomforts there may be specific remedies, but often skilled nursing brings the greatest relief. It has already been stated that severe breathlessness in the dying person can be very difficult to treat. Nursing a breathless person so that he is comfortable, free from restlessness and positioned so that he can expand his chest fully, may well relieve most of the sense of suffocation. Oxygen may help if it can be given without the patient feeling that the apparatus appears to restrict or crowd in upon him. Some minor surgical procedures, such as removing fluid that has collected round the lung, and some medicines may improve the remaining function of lung or heart a little. If there is a useless persistent cough, this can be quieted. As the end of life draws closer still, morphia or heroin can ease the struggle for breath.

The relief of the physical discomforts of the dying by nursing techniques and suitable medicines can only be mentioned briefly in this book. Nausea and vomiting can be eased by nursing a person in bed and choosing the appropriate times to encourage him to take suitable drinks, suck ice or take some food. Some of the fairly recent anti-emetic drugs are usually effective in relieving much of this unpleasant symptom of sickness. Bladder or bowel malfunction can be dealt with through skilled nursing attention and simple equipment to help regular emptying without in-continence. The use of catheters to drain the bladder has now been made easier since more recent appliances can be placed and left in position without their giving rise to complications. These measures together with prompt, unfussed changing of bedclothes when normal control is lost occasionally, ease physical or psychological distress. Efficient nursing will add greatly to the ill person's comfort by routine hygienic measures started in good time. It is often possible to prevent the mouth from getting unpleasantly dry and sore. It is important to guard against the risk of bed-sores, which develop when unaccustomed parts of a poorly nourished body take continuous pressure in bed. The bed-ridden must be helped to change position regularly and the skin kept clean and dry.

As well as skill in nursing techniques, to tend dying people requires a readiness to give devoted, perhaps continuous, care combined with mental flexibility in pursuing the aim of bringing comfort. Treating some incidental thing like a sore toe may bring as much relief as a lot of attention to the fatal illness. Insomnia need not be automatically met by the administration of barbiturates. Sleep may be induced more satisfactorily by paying attention to physical comfort and the ritual of settling for the night, perhaps with a pleasant drink, alcoholic or otherwise. If a sedative drug is necessary, however, it should be used without hesitation. If nurses and doctors set about to relieve discomfort with sincerity and competence, their intention alone brings ease.

CARE FOR THE WHOLE PERSON

The physical methods of helping a dying person's discomfort are of the greatest importance and there are many excellent writings on these matters,[173, 214, 61] but the incurable patient needs not only efficient practical care but faith in the judgement of those who must advise on his whole treatment programme. Will the doctor, using his knowledge of treating disease, come to a balanced judgement between the striving for cure and the seeking of his patient's comfort? Will he advise with understanding on the question of care at home or in hospital? Is the doctor's philosophy at odds with the outlook of the dying person, or are their views at least compatible over what things are important when life is drawing to a close? When there is no trust given or deserved, the dying person has a considerable added burden.

It is important for the patient to know that his doctor holds a sober balance between the need to investigate all aspects of a disease and the need to accept some illness as incurable. He will not wish the doctor to miss opportunities of cure, but neither will he want to endure unnecessary discomfort and disappointment in pursuing will-o'-the-wisps. If it is not clear beyond reasonable doubt that the condition is certain to be a fatal one, the doctor has to decide how much investigating is warranted before being satisfied that the evidence for a fatal outcome is sufficient. An increasing demand of sound judgement is needed now that medical ingenuity has made possible a host of special examinations of parts of the body formerly thought inaccessible, and devised innumerable tests of functions that were once unknown. Occasionally a dying person will need the doctor to protect him from the zeal of his relatives who want to leave no possibility untried. It may be appropriate to explain to them that it is unnecessary, even unkind, to seek further to avoid the obvious conclusion that the patient cannot be cured. The anxieties of relatives should be helped so that they do not seek the outlet of fruitless medical activities or press for troublesome investigations and treatments which can do no good. It is not usually justified to give a dying person a quite irrational untried treatment just in case there is a miraculous cure. After a short while of spurious hope there is the bitter anti-climax when all proves to have been in vain.

The absence of affection and trust between dying patients and those who look after them will vitiate the potential benefits of scientific skill. Technical achievements alone, although great, are not always sufficient to banish all discomfort. They may fail because the only available treatments have their own unwanted effects; for example, it may occasionally require so much of a drug to make a person entirely free of all pain that the drug itself will render him semi-conscious or nauseated. Sometimes the patient would prefer to have a little discomfort and remain alert enough to enjoy the visits of friends and to participate in the life of those about him.[176] He can tolerate a little pain if he feels confident in the people caring for him, if he is sure that they are concerned for his comfort and have regard for him as an individual. Perhaps this valuable relationship can be at its best between a patient and his trusted family doctor. It is almost inconceivable that the relationship between a doctor and a dying patient can remain impersonal. Even if a doctor assumes that he is impersonal in his approach to a problem of disease and judges the matter accordingly, the patient will regard this attitude in a very personal way. How can a person during his last days on earth be cared for adequately if there is not some intuitive sympathetic understanding of how he feels?

To treat the patient with incurable illness properly, it is necessary to bear in mind that each added symptom carries further implications for the sick person. Each capacity that is weakened and lost through the illness means that less independence is left. Every fresh symptom is another encroachment upon the diminishing reserve of health that stands between him and death. Each perceptible deterioration may renew the emotional conflict felt over the struggle against the disease or the resignation to die. With this grim importance, symptoms may not be easily dispelled. Nurses and doctors should, by their attitude, avoid worsening these partially relieved symptoms and their symbolic significance by neither ignoring nor exaggerating their importance. If a dying person's symptoms are only given perfunctory attention he may experience desolation out of proportion to the apparent disregard.

Ill people gain help when someone simply pays attention to their complaints, even if they have described them several times before. Telling itself brings ease, and what is told will often indicate untried ways of bringing comfort. One bed-ridden patient, obviously ill, who had a number of cancerous deposits in different parts of her body, continued to complain a good deal in spite of the fact that most of her pain had been relieved. Among other manifestations of her disease, one of the nerves to her eye had been affected to cause a squint; it could not be restored to normal. The medical staff were apt to be more aware of the importance of this abnormality as a sign of the cancer spread, but she wanted to describe at some length how she felt about having a squint and seeing double – what would people think of her appearance, would her sight get worse? She could not truthfully be told it would get better, but some of her fears about her vision could be discounted. Just allowing her to speak more fully of the matter, letting her know that those looking after her realized how she felt, was sufficient for her to feel better; and a patch over one eye enabled her to see and read quite well again without the troublesome double image. This is a very ordinary example of the sympathetic help that the incurably ill need and will get if nursing and medical staff have the time and motivation to give it.

This leads on to another aspect of symptoms; they should not always be accepted just at their face value. Sometimes a person cannot really tell what is troubling him and his body 'voices' his distress. In ordinary life, the person who is anxious and tense over something indefinable, may experience a headache and at first may complain only of that sensation and not his worry. When a dying person tells his doctor of a physical symptom, sometimes, given sufficient time to tell, he may alter the nature of his initial complaint. He is ill and troubled and can perhaps most easily put his first appeal as a mention of pain. He may make it quite clear that he does indeed experience a definite pain. Sometimes, however, the description of pain and discomfort is elaborated further until the listener, and perhaps the speaker, become aware that it is not so much a pain, but the emotional distress over the situation which needs relief. The distress may be his fearful uncertainty over what will happen to him. Unsure of what he may be doomed to suffer, present minor symptoms become inescapable anguish. The dying patient is not malingering when he complains of physical discomforts which do not seem to be solely due to his physical disease. He is genuinely troubled by sensations he experiences. They may be allayed when he can view them in the right perspective, and that requires some measure of confidence.

The tormenting uncertainty of the dying may be that inherent in the thought of life's end. Often it is not so general, but a more accessible uncertainty focused on practical considerations. Questions loom large in his mind, such as what care he will have while the disease is ending his life. We are fortunate in Great Britain that the dying person does not have to fear that the cost of his medical treatment is any bar to his seeking help. In many poorer countries, adequate treatment cannot be afforded by a large proportion of the populace. Even in much more advanced countries, the insurance schemes may not cover a long illness and the patient often fears that his treatment may beggar his family. It may even contribute to a delay in getting medical advice on serious disease. For instance, in North America, a study of a group of patients who had delayed seeking treatment for tumours revealed that a quarter felt that expense had been their main deterrent.[76] It is not easy to give the most efficacious help to patients in this state of mind.

Reassurance comes to the dying if it is clearly demonstrated that nurses and doctors have every intention of controlling discomfort. For instance, if there is pain it should be clearly mastered. This is best done by regular doses of sufficient analgesics given in good time before the discomfort returns. Then the ill person is not haunted by the thought that the pain may soon return, requiring him to decide whether to hang on as long as possible or ask for relief with the first warning twinge, the coming of which is awaited. To give analgesics to patients with painful incurable disease only when the pain gets bad, means that they are inevitably going to spend part of their day in pain, waiting for the next lot of drugs to work. When all severe pain is banished by regular repeated medicines, the troubled patient realizes that he will be able to face with some dignity the remaining portion of life: his returning courage will ease or even banish symptoms that formerly were so troublesome.

Besides the security of knowing that he will not be broken down by intolerable suffering, the dying person needs assurance that he can be adequately tended if he becomes quite weak or helpless. If he is fortunate, there may be a relative or someone near to him who is quite able and very willing to give all the nursing help and whatever else is necessary. This is not always so, sometimes there is no one. Sometimes the care becomes too much; the patient and his amateur nurse get increasingly perturbed as they realize the situation is getting out of hand. When some sympathetic and efficient professional nursing help is added, the result can be dramatic. With some deft nursing or immediate understanding of need, a nurse can restore order, calm and therefore comfort, where there was incipient panic and discomfort. If attention to personal cleanliness has become impossible, the nurse's restoration of habitual cleanliness and neatness allows self-esteem to return. For the exhausted person, uncomfortable and sore in a bed that seems strangely corrugated, an adjustment of the bedclothes and his position shows that comfort can be obtained. Such measures, without fussing, push much insecurity away and destroy the seed of fearful agony that lies in every growing discomfort.

HELPING THE EMOTIONALLY DISTRESSED

If, together with adequate physical care, the dying person had sufficient human companionship, most of his anguish would be prevented. He wants to see and know that those about him still have a warm interest in himself. Even if there is a painful recognition that his working life and consequent status among his fellows have come to an end, he wants to know that personal ties remain.[176] Unfortunately, this is not always so and a dying person can suffer from the impression that he is written off and already being forgotten. Occasionally a patient feels this so much as to say that people already seem to act as if he were dead. In pleasant company he is less likely to have his fears grow too big and overwhelming, apprehensions not only for himself but also for those he loves.

The relatives and friends of the dying patient may not be able to give the supportive companionship or nursing care that they would like to give if they themselves are troubled. They may need help to cope with the situation and their own feelings. A host of emotions can flood over them, from panic to avarice, guilt to grief. The nature of these feelings depends in part on how they had previously got on with the dying person. Those with close emotional ties will probably experience much sorrow – not always in proportion to the outward show of affection that had formerly existed. They are

likely to be anxious over the suffering and disability the ill person
may experience, perhaps overwhelmed with the thought that the
fatal illness will be quite unlike any other illness that they have
nursed the person through before. This may lead them to give up
prematurely any thought of caring for the ill person and to
withdraw from the situation in helpless discomfiture. In their uncertainty they may ask the doctor for impossibly definite pre-
dictions, about events not wholly foreseeable: how long has he got
to live, what will be the course of the illness and so on. Throughout the family there will be a sense of loss and of being lost. If they
can talk easily about their problems or know they can reach the
sympathetic ear of a competent person also involved in the care of
the one they love, their own sense of insecurity will be eased. There
is a self-questioning, common to many situations of loss or
approaching loss. Can they do anything more to help, or, more
despairingly, could they have done more?

If the family can have help and sympathy when they need it, the
dying person in turn will reap considerable benefit. He is usually
immensely concerned over the family he is about to leave. He will
want to know, preferably directly from them, that they are self-
supporting or that someone has adequately taken over both small
and great duties that he thought essential. If they seem secure, then
the dying person is less troubled. Together with an altruistic feeling for them, he still wants to know what is happening in their life
and to be part of it. The obvious solution of many of the doubts is
for the dying person to stay at home with his family participating
in his care. This may take place as a matter of course. In some cases
with sufficient guidance and encouragement relatives may undertake nursing tasks that they did not feel themselves capable of, and
thereby obtain some sense of fulfilment. They will be able to
manage with greater confidence if they know that more skilled
hands are ready to take over in the terminal phase should the
demands of nursing become too great. As long as the relatives
can do most of the nursing without it getting beyond their capa-
bilities, their strength or their limits of confidence, then the united
feeling within the family will help the dying person keep undue fear
and grief at bay.

The personal support given to the dying by relatives, friends, priest, nurses or doctor will either come intuitively or through their constant alertness for any sign that the patient has a need for spiritual comfort. Often the only necessity is just their willingness to spend some time with the dying. Perhaps we are less good at ungrudgingly giving our time to people nowadays. There comes a stage when those not in the immediate family, visitors, doctors, and nurses, do not need to do much, but just to be available. Reasonably frequent unhurried visits, coupled with a willingness to take oneself off when unwanted, can bring great comfort to the ill person and his family. The dying person may have moments of anguish, especially when he does not want to die. Then someone who is fond of him, or even the compassionate nurse, may well have the spontaneous human impulse to hold on to him, and with their touch give comfort as death draws nearer.

If anguish is severe or long-lasting, further help may be necessary. There are times when simple care and understanding are insufficient to prevent a dying person from being swamped by fear and misery. Often the commonly used sedatives and tranquillizing drugs may relieve the panic or the preoccupation with dismal thoughts. The last ten or twenty years has seen a considerable advance in the effectiveness of drugs to counter fear, agitation and depression, and they can often do this without making the person particularly drowsy.[84] If these do not prove sufficient, drugs like heroin and cocaine can be given. It is not uncommon to see someone whose remaining days of life were being made unbearable by apprehension and grief, brought to peace, even tinctured with a little consoling hope, by judicious use of these drugs. Many examples of this effect could be given, and it is almost standard practice in some hospitals. Take the case of one man who was dying of cancer and having a hard time during his last illness. The disease was giving him some pain and it also affected his nervous system, causing an increasing paralysis and inability to pass water. For some days he was very unhappy, he spoke of the fact that he was dying and felt hopeless and helpless and unable to do anything about it. Within a short while of starting regular morphia and cocaine his spirits rose. He allowed himself to have the touch of hope for recovery that he so much wanted. He remained in this happier state until passing into the comatose condition that preceded his death some days later.

Such drugs are of great assistance, but it often seems more appropriate to help the frightened or depressed to find within themselves the means of overcoming their emotional distress, especially if death is still some way off. It is not often that psychiatrists are consulted over the care of a distressed dying person, perhaps because the patient's wretchedness seems so understandable when he is suffering from an incurable disease; but in some cases psychiatrists' particular experience could be useful. They are practised in eliciting the causes of people's distress and have developed the skill of hearing the emotionally relevant aspects of halting or circumlocutory accounts.

People in mental distress often get sufficient help from just an undirected outpouring of troubles and a sharing of grief. In some cases it may prove more helpful to use some form of psychotherapy to guide a person towards considering some of the likely sources of his mental discomfort. If the patient wishes, it will probably be relevant to discuss not only his suspicion or belief that he is dying but how he views this prospect. The fact that he will soon be dead may trouble him far less than some of the particular consequences of being a dying person. He may be distressed and frustrated by the taboo-like avoidance of any thought or mention of dying, when he is well aware that his life is ending. Perhaps he will not wish to say much of the fact that he will not recover, but he wants at least some tacit understanding that it is so. He is very likely to be troubled if other people withdraw from him, as they may do, because he is a dying man. A psychotherapist may also detect and perhaps help distress which stems from lifelong features of character, such as a chronic feeling of personal failure or a continuous burden of real or imagined guilt. It may be possible to give support to the emotionally insecure person who, as he is dying, can be greatly troubled when deprived of his former over-treasured apparent ability to control his own life, or misses too much his sense of being useful or indispensable; these losses produce in him, while life is finishing, a sense of fear and worthlessness.[165]

While a psychiatrist – or for that matter, any other person – is getting to know how a patient feels, he will probably build up a valuable rapport with the dying person. To achieve more than a superficial harmony, there will probably need to be some mutual admission, even if tacit, that the condition is not benign. For the patient's sake, the psychiatrist will probably want his treatment to be conducted in an atmosphere of friendly understanding and trust. Perhaps it should be said that in psychotherapy in other circumstances, a patient may sometimes usefully express criticism and anger towards his doctor, unwittingly transferring for a while these negative feelings, which originate from other sources, to the person who is treating him. In the dying, although these negative feelings may arise and be discussed, the psychotherapist is likely to encourage a positive feeling of goodwill between them. He may well allow more of his own warmth and liking for the patient to become apparent than is usual in some conventions of psychotherapy.[141]

The part that psychotherapy can usefully play in patients distressed during their terminal illness is still relatively unknown. It can be valuable. It can undoubtedly throw a considerable strain upon the psychotherapist himself. This sense of strain and involvement is understandable of course, and should be acceptable as long as the psychotherapist does not become so identified with the patient as to himself manifest such anxiety and sadness that it impairs the quality of help he can give to the dying person.[47] Those embarking on the rewarding but potentially stressful personal treatment of dying people should be alert to any circumstances that might lead to a premature break in a close relationship, which could add to a patient's distress.[43]

The priest has a more traditional and, for some people, an essential part to play in preparing a person for death. As minister and as man he can give great comfort to the dying patient. Often he is hurriedly sent for when it is too late for him to give the spiritual comfort that he might well have conveyed. There is much to be said for a doctor, or someone who knows of the patient's fatal illness, inquiring after his religious views and, when it is indicated, discussing the situation with the clergyman before the patient fully realizes or is told that he is dying. Then the minister can give continued help to the patient and his family as long as it is needed.[72] He can speak with greater authority to the dying and assure him that whatever happens after this life ends, God will be there to receive him, perhaps asserting that the Lord is forgiving.[10]

The dying person will often wish to prepare himself spiritually for approaching death and will need the priest for this. In the religious faith of some dying people it is most important for them to take a conscious part in a preparatory service. The Last Sacraments of the Roman Catholic with Penance, Viaticum and Extreme Unction warn and prepare a patient for the end of his mortal life. Roman Catholic priests are concerned that those in their mortal illness should be aware that they are about to die. Individual priests will speak to the dying with varying degrees of certainty and gentleness about the possible advent of death. Most clergymen of any denomination will, of course, prefer to be able to speak to the one who is about to die about this essential fact. This raises the whole question of whether the dying can be helped as much as they should if the fatal nature of their condition is never mentioned.

10 Speaking of Death with the Dying

The frequently debated question, 'Should the doctor tell?', tends to carry a false implication that the doctor knows all about the patient's approaching death and the patient knows nothing. The resultant discussion and controversy is therefore often irrelevant or, at least, tangential to the real problem. Doctors are far from omniscient. Even if they have no doubt that their patients' condition will be fatal, they can rarely foretell the time of death with any accuracy unless it is close at hand. Furthermore, as we have seen, patients are not necessarily unaware of what is happening; many have a very clear idea that they are dying.

Rather than putting a choice between telling or not telling, it would be more useful to ask other questions. Should we encourage or divert a patient who begins to speak of matters that will lead to talk of dying? How freely should we speak to him about it? Should we lie to him if we suspect he only wants to be told that all will be well? If he sincerely wishes to know if his illness will be fatal, should his suppositions be confirmed? If he never asks outright, have we a duty to tell him? Is it right to deny knowledge of dying to those who ask or wrong to tell those who show no wish to know? Should we allow the awareness of dying to grow gradually, or should patients who are mortally ill know this early on, so that they may attain greater acceptance of dying? If they are to be told more openly, how should such knowledge be given? How do people react to being told? These questions, all part of that oversimplified, 'Should the doctor tell?', can have no universally accepted answer. Individuals differ and ethical beliefs or current opinions will influence judgement.

TO SPEAK FREELY?

There are some good reasons for speaking freely about the possibility of dying to those with fatal conditions. An ill person who strongly suspects that he is dying, but is denied the least opportunity to question or discuss this, can feel cruelly isolated if he does not want this conspiracy of silence. He may be surrounded by people whose every manifest word or action is designed to deny or avoid the fact that he is dying, and he is aware of the artificiality of their deception. How can he gain the ease of wholly sincere talk with others if all maintain the pretence that his imminent departure from life, his leaving them for ever, is just not taking place? It would be thought preposterous and cruel if throughout a mother's first pregnancy and delivery all around conspired to treat it as indigestion and never gave her an opportunity to voice her doubts.

The view that we have a duty to inform the dying man has some support on material and spiritual grounds. If a doctor conceals from a patient that he is mortally ill, the person may fail to order his family affairs or may embark on business ventures which he would not contemplate if he knew his likely fate. The doctor's legal responsibility to warn the dying person appears to be a matter of debate. Most doctors however will bear in mind how far a person needs to set his affairs in order, when considering what they should tell a dying patient. Imparting advice to a man that it might be a wise precaution to tidy up business arrangements serves more than that single function.[103] Conveyed with tact, it is a hint that an ill man can discuss further with his doctor if he is of a mind to know more, or it is advice he can just accept at its face value.

The spiritual need for a man to know that he is dying may well take precedence over material matters in the terminal phase. Frequently the dying person spontaneously turns or returns to his religious beliefs. He may already have prayed for help in his serious illness, perhaps with rather unfamiliar voice. If it appears that recovery is unlikely, most ministers hold strongly that the patient should know this, so that he can prepare for eternal life.

At times there is an increasing need to be frank with a patient over his prognosis, because he has short periods of feverish hopes followed by long periods of despairing misery. He may waste effort and money on unjustified and quite hopeless treatments, only to have bitter disappointment as proclaimed panaceas fail. If a patient is seriously ill and appears to be getting worse, while his physician appears content with ineffective remedies, he may feel that opportunities of cure are being lost. This may lead to a feeling of frustration or a desperate tour of other doctors. Of course, a second opinion from a respected source may be a great help to all concerned. This may bring assurance that no important possibility is being neglected. When a troubled patient who has been seeking fruitlessly for cure comes to a better understanding with his doctor on the nature of his disease and how much hope is justifiable, he may regain confidence and find greater peace.

In spite of these arguments which favour frankness with the dying, many doctors are reluctant to speak with them of death. They feel that most patients do not wish to raise the subject except to get reassurance, and that the truth is likely to be hurtful. This common medical attitude is uncomfortably combined with a considerable hesitation over practising deliberate evasion and deceit on patients who have put their trust in the doctor, even if the 'white lies' are intended to avoid distress. Some forthright physicians, however, make plain their belief that it does patients no good to be told that they are dying.[9] It is a viewpoint easy to attack on theoretical grounds; but when truth can give rise to considerable distress, when kindly half-truths do not materially alter the course to death and when dying people would like to hear that they will recover, it takes a very convinced man to condemn evasion or even the occasional untruth. Many scrupulous people who care for the dying find themselves concealing the truth in a manner they always wished to avoid.

In practice relatively few doctors tell patients that there is no hope of recovery. In one study of medical opinion, for example, a group of over two hundred doctors, working in hospital and private practice, were asked if they favoured informing those

patients found to have a cancer very likely to prove fatal.[143]
Patients so defined would include, of course, some whose symptoms were investigated early while they were in reasonable general
health with death some way off. Such patients might have little
reason at this stage to suspect their illness to be mortal and if a
doctor did tell them, it would give some unanticipated bad news.
Eighty-eight per cent of these doctors would not tell the patient,
although some of them would make exceptions. The doctors felt
that usually the patient's questions were pleas for reassurance.
The other 12 per cent usually told the patients that they had
cancer especially if the latter were intelligent and emotionally
stable. Most of the doctors felt that they should inform a relative
and were glad to share the burden of their knowledge. Incidentally
no less than 60 per cent of these same doctors said that they
would like to be told if they themselves had an equally sinister
form of cancer. This inconsistency of opinion between imparting
and receiving such information was explained by the doctors on
the basis of their own greater fortitude or responsibilities. It might
be so, but it is more likely to be the emotionally determined
attitude found among lay and medical people alike. This was
indicated by the fact that these physicians were not any more
frank with doctors whom they treated for cancer than any other
patients with cancer.

The reluctance to admit to a sick person that his illness may be
fatal is not confined to physicians. One survey of people's wishes
to be told if they had cancer indicated that they themselves would
prefer to be told but were less in favour of recommending that
others in a similar condition should be informed.[101] In the study
of terminal care in Britain by Cartwright and Anderson the
relatives and friends of the deceased appeared to know more and
expected to be told more than the dying person about his true
condition. About half of these patients were aware of their
condition. Although many of the informants in this study accepted
the degree of either knowledge or ignorance shown by the dying,
there was stronger approval of the patient not knowing than of
his being aware.[36] During a current inquiry into the way married
people cope with one partner's fatal illness, it appears that hardly

a quarter openly discuss their mutual situation even though tacit understanding may be there.

Although the majority of practising doctors may believe that it is better for them to be reticent with the dying, this opinion must be reconsidered in the light of the fact than an equally large proportion of lay people say that they would like to be told. On the surface, it seems quite perverse that 80 or 90 per cent of physicians say that they rarely, if ever, tell patients that their illness is mortal,[143] whereas about 80 per cent of patients say they would like to be told.[64] If a doctor sees the question in rather unreal black-and-white terms of either pressing unpleasant news of impending death upon a patient or keeping him in happy ignorance of his fate, this will sway him towards expressing an opinion against telling. This travesties the usual situation, however, where the dying person, with gathering doubts and clues, becomes increasingly suspicious that his condition is mortal.

It is often suggested that the very high percentage of people who give the theoretical answer that they would like to know if they had cancer, do so because they feel secure in their present state of good health. They might be less confident if there was an immediate possibility of having a fatal illness. Albeit, almost as high a proportion of patients actually being treated for cancer in Manchester were just as much in favour of being told of their diagnosis.[3] They had been told they had a treatable cancer and later on were asked if they approved or disapproved of being informed. Two thirds were glad to have been told, only 7 per cent disapproved and 19 per cent denied having been told – the familiar phenomenon of failing to hear or remember what one does not wish to learn. This particular group of patients, however, had curable cancers. Is it the same for those with incurable cancers?

The answer appears to be that they equally wish to know. In the University Hospitals at Minnesota it is the practice of doctors to tell their patients the diagnosis.[64] A group of patients with advanced cancer were asked if they knew their diagnosis and 86 per cent did know. Most had been told by their doctor, although some found out in other ways. Many of the remaining 14 per cent, who did not know, had asked at one time and been given evasive answers. As many as four fifths of these very ill patients thought that cancer patients should be told. They said it had helped them understand their own illness and given them peace of mind. It also allowed them to plan for further medical care, religious matters and for other aspects of their families and their own lives.

HOW TO SPEAK OF DYING?

There are, therefore, several good reasons justifying considerable candour with people who are fatally ill. If this were to be more widely accepted in principle, how and when should such sincere conversation take place? Clearly an abrupt statement to every patient with incurable disease that he is going to die is likely to do more harm than good.

Some wish to know only a little of their illness. As with non-fatal disease a person may be helped by simple explanations of the illness, together with a general plan of investigating or treating the condition. An intelligent young woman, who was admitted to hospital with an obviously growing lump on one rib, was very troubled while investigations were done and treatment started without anyone telling her what it was. There was not much reassuring information to give her, as it was the sign of a widespread cancer. She wanted to know something, however. She was told that it was a tumour and that the X-rays had shown up one or two smaller ones. They would be treated by radiotherapy and, it was correctly said, her condition would improve considerably. This was as much as she wanted to know at that time. She had been very anxious, but after this talk she was less so. She was quite sad for a day or two, and then her spirits recovered. This sort of response of sorrow on learning of having serious disease, followed by greater equanimity as acceptance grows, is the usual understandable reaction.

Some dying patients want to know even less than this sort of edited version of the truth. They may not want to hear a word about the nature of their condition. They may well have a hidden suspicion and gladly enter a tacit conspiracy to avoid the whole subject. They wish others to take over all responsibilities, anxieties, and decisions. This total surrender of all decision to the doctor may be somewhat less common now, especially as doctors tend to lose a little of their former authoritative manner and more patients refuse to put up with it. But when seriously ill, it can be easier for a patient to relinquish all control, all knowledge, to his doctor. If the dying person indicates openly that he does not want to know, if he shows by his manner or by his talk that he does not wish to regard his illness as fatal, it would be uncharitable to force the truth upon him. The aim is to make dying a little easier, not to apply a dogma of always divulging truth.[5]

It is not an easy problem when a patient asks about his incurable illness in a way that indicates his need for reassurance or, at least, hope. He is probably more likely to ask such questions as 'It's not cancer, is it, doctor?' if his doctor has shown no sign of giving any spontaneous comment about his condition. If a patient does blurt out this loaded question, or suddenly asks, 'Will I get better?', of someone ill-prepared to answer, the situation is potentially distressing to both. The result is often a hasty untruthful re-assurance. If this is given in an atmosphere of doubt and anxiety, present in both their minds, little good will be done to the ill person's morale. If the question has been met with a hasty denial or a misleadingly optimistic view, this may be accepted with gratitude. Sometimes it is taken as a more definite answer than was intended. The ill person may even, by a series of further questions, based on the first slanted answer, wring out a more emphatic denial of fatal disease than one would wish to give. This is disturbing, but is not necessarily a catastrophe, even if the patient later comes to realize that his first misgivings were well-founded. Nevertheless, an emotional balance achieved on a basis of assurances bound to be proved false, is no stable adjustment. When the original loaded question is put, it is often better not to answer the dying person's anxious inquiry straight away. Returning the question, asking him to describe more fully what anxieties he has in mind and listening sympathetically to his doubts and fears will meet some of his needs. Then the fuller description may show the basis of his anxiety. It may be a totally unwarranted fear which can be allayed, such as an anticipation of prolonged agony. It may be a well-founded apprehension, but one that can be borne with help. In the long run, especially if there is someone at hand to help with any subsequent doubts, allowing a person to discuss his fears may prove more valuable than a hasty, consoling, but untrue, answer.

In practice, probably the best and easiest way to broach the matter of dying with a mortally ill person is just to allow him to speak of his suspicions or knowledge of the outcome. If necessary, he can be asked how he feels and shown that more than the polite stereotyped answer is wanted. The mention of worry allows an invitation to talk unhurriedly of the troubling prospect.[43] Then frequently the doctor will find that there is little for him to 'tell', all that is required is for him to listen with sympathy. In these circumstances the dying person does not usually ask for reassurance or praise for his courage. He may glance up for confirmation of mutual understanding. He may want to know a little more to clarify some aspect of the situation. It is quite possible for the doctor to be uncertain of the exact course of an illness and yet, when asked, to give an honest qualified answer without lying or undue prevarication. To many people this brings firmer comfort than the flimsy props of obviously false promises or the chaos of apparently bewildered ignorance. In treating any disease it is common enough to be thinking in terms of probabilities and possibilities rather than certainties. As compensation for our having to endure uncertainty, it is uncommon to be in a position where there is no comforting straw of hope for survival.

If it is unclear if an ill person desires to know the whole truth, it is possible to start by giving gentle hints. A simple explanation of the disease, mentioning the favourable aspects of treatment and touching upon the other serious possibilities, will enable the ill person to take up the aspects he wishes and ignore others.[4] The beginnings of awareness may be started early. A surgeon before operating upon a suspected cancer will often tell the patient that if the condition is serious he will need to perform an extensive operation. The patient who has such an operation can then pursue the matter with the doctor as much as he wishes. He can apprehend

the threat of the illness, or concentrate on the curative value of
the treatment.

Many doctors prefer to use an oblique approach of letting the
patient know that he may be dying. Without any deception or lies,
they aim to allow an awareness of the outcome to grow. If need be
a germ of realization is planted, but hope is never utterly excluded.
Discussion can be reasonably frank, but the emphasis is on the
favourable aspects.[62] If, indeed, the awareness of dying is going to
grow, those who care for the patient must be prepared to keep
pace with this increasing realization. They should be ready to
listen and let the patient know that some of his surmises are true
and some of his fears are unjustified. In this way the dying person
should not feel too lonely, too uncertain, nor plunged into acute
emotional distress. If the doctor concerned has cared for the
patient for some years, then he should have a background knowledge of the individual which can guide how much should be said
and when, Logically enough, if anyone does talk to the patient
of his condition, more often than not it will be his general
practitioner.[36]

Although it is not an infallible guide to how much the dying
patient should be told, his apparent wishes and questions do point
the way. This means that the manner in which he puts his views
should be closely attended to – the intonations and the exact
wording may be very revealing. It also means that he must be
given ample opportunity to express his ideas and ask his questions.
If the questions are sincere, however, then why not give quiet
straight answers to the patient's questions about his illness and
the outcome? It makes for beneficial trust.[114]

It is to be remembered that while doctors are trying to judge
their patients' capacity to stand unpleasant news, many patients
are equally making their intuitive judgements of whether their
doctor can bear sincere but difficult questions. They often have a
very accurate idea of which doctor is quite unaccustomed or unsuited to being frank about fatal illness to the person most concerned. I have often been told by understanding people, towards
the end of their life, that they knew that the doctor looking after
them could not easily talk about this. 'He feels he's got to get

people well and I couldn't very well talk to him about not getting better,' said a woman who knew she would soon die. If a patient is firmly insistent and his doctor is honest, frank conversations do take place. 'I asked him what they'd found and then I asked him if it was cancer. And now I know it's cancer and they haven't been able to take it all away. There's only one in a thousand chance of recovery.' The physician who had been questioned by this man said that he felt that he had probably been more perturbed by the conversation than the patient had.

In the care of children there is an even greater reluctance and sense of concern over any mention to them of dying. It seems clear that some children are well aware that they may be dying and they may well be perturbed by the altered behaviour of their parents.[218] If they make any suggestion to adults that they may not recover, almost inevitably they will be greeted by 'reassurance'. If another child in the ward dies there is usually a pretence that this was not so. Undoubtedly, like adults, not all children necessarily want to consider explicitly the likelihood of dying. A change in their behaviour or a denying of obvious symptoms may be a clue to the fears they hide. Very few people feel adequate to coping with frank conversation with a dying child, although we may wonder how lonely they may be feeling.[28] Some have managed this, perhaps more easily when religious conviction is there, and diminished the child's sense of isolation.

Occasionally those concerned with a patient's care hold conflicting views over his need to be told. Such unpleasant disagreements, when they do occur, are not resolved as often as they should be by discovering what the patient already knows. Nor do those with his interest at heart meet as often as they should to see what common ground they have between their seemingly opposed and entrenched beliefs.

It is perhaps strange that there is so much more agreement over talking frankly to members of the family about their relative's fatal illness rather than to the patient himself, even if he shows a wish to know. It reverses the usual convention of the doctor keeping confidential the information concerning an adult and telling other people only if the patient agrees. A few doctors, if they tell the patient the serious nature of the illness, do discuss with them who else should be informed. Usually the next of kin is told, but often it is clear that some other responsible member of the family is better able to receive the information and pass on the appropriate knowledge to the rest. As with the patient, the families receiving these tidings often need more than just a bulletin of bad news. Many cannot take in the shattering information at first.[86] Time and much troubled thought is needed before people can accept that someone they love is about to die. They may well need help.

REACTIONS TO SPEAKING OF DEATH

Many patients have said what a relief they have felt when at last they have had a chance to talk openly about the probability that they are dying.[106] As so many gain comfort from this, it is clearly unkind to deny them the opportunity. They do not get the chance because people are fearful of embarking on such conversations. In the book *Awareness of Dying* by Glaser and Strauss,[65] the authors refer to the fact that some people who care for patients are recognized by their colleagues to have an aptitude for speaking easily and honestly to the dying, and bring them comfort. I am sure that many more people could do this if the climate of opinion changed towards greater frankness, and more people realized how much they could help in this way. Most nurses, medical students, and young doctors do not receive as much help as they should, during their training, over the problems raised in caring for the dying.

If more people become prepared to speak freely with the dying there will be a need for caution, because although many would benefit, some would react adversely. A proportion of people, nearing the end of life, are very distressed by implicit or explicit references to death's coming. A little exploratory conversation may indicate a patient's likely reaction. He may say quite clearly what he wants. A man who was pretty sure that he had abdominal cancer said, 'I want them to tell me if they *are* going to operate. If they aren't, I want them to give me the wire. Then I'll know what to make of it.' It was clear that he was not one who only wanted to know as long as the news was good.

There can be some intuitive judgement of how much particular individuals should be told. Their habitual manner of dealing with life can be a useful guide, their style of facing former difficulties or attaining their social position.[142] This was illustrated by one equable man who had risen to a responsible position supervising a group of shops. He had always coped well with problems in life, once he knew what was needed to be done. The previous year he had had a kidney removed and had been told that all should be well after the operation. His wife, however, had been told that he had a cancer and also warned, according to his doctor's usual policy, not to tell the patient. When the patient entered hospital again with a spread of his cancer, he insisted on being told the true state of affairs. He took it very well, but regretted that he had not been told before, so that he and his wife could have openly acknowledged that he might have little time to live. Naturally, a patient's expressed wishes and clues from his past life as to his manner of facing difficulties give no perfect prediction. The man who has succeeded in life, developing strong friendships and warm family ties may, in spite of his apparent stability, be unable to cope with the threat of so much loss. The less happy person may be better prepared to give up his life.[4] Nevertheless, the view that a stable person will probably retain this characteristic when facing death usually proves correct.

In general, learning that an illness is likely to be fatal produces a period of disquiet, even dismay, although this may be effectively concealed. However well the knowledge has been conveyed, it is almost bound to cause some emotional reaction. If frank discussions were often to result in patients becoming severely or persistently distressed, even suicidal, few doctors would wish to speak to them of dying. There does tend to be an exaggerated fear that dying patients will kill themselves if they are told that their illness may be fatal. The chances are that the suicidal acts which occur in those with mortal disease are due to the suffering and the spiritual isolation when the sick are lonely, rather than any despair following a sympathetic discussion of their outlook. Although suicide remains a threatening possibility, inhibiting some from frank discussion with the dying, it is hard to find a case where a humane conversation on these lines precipitated any suicidal act. It is much more likely to have prevented it. 'I knew what I'd got,' said a young woman who had attempted suicide, 'I'd seen it in my notes. I'd looked it up in the medical books and I knew I couldn't recover. I wanted to talk about it with the doctor, but he always seemed too busy, or just called it inflammation.'

Clumsy telling of a fatal illness can cause great distress, but this extreme is generally avoidable. There is an account of one Veterans' Administration Hospital in North America where it was the practice to tell the patient the nature of his illness, including fatal illness.[65] Many of the patients in this hospital were from a low social class or destitute, and, it seems, not necessarily treated with much dignity. Some of the doctors made a practice of short, blunt announcements to the patients and walking away. Some softened it a little and assured the patient that pain would be controlled. Although they could justify telling the truth because the patients become 'philosophical' about it after a few days, this technique seems hard. The sociologists describing the situation wrote that the abrupt disclosure tended to result in a more immediate profound depression. As a result the patients were more apt to try and cope with such potential distress by denying the reality of their situation, rather than being helped to accept it.

In order to evaluate more reliably the effect of telling patients that they have a mortal illness, a careful and courageous investigation was carried out by some of the medical staff at Lund University.[63] Some patients with an incurable illness were told and others were not. Personal contact was maintained throughout the further course and treatment of their illness, taking care to note if the greater frankness or reticence was more helpful to them. A psychiatrist made a preliminary assessment of the patients to see if there were any indications of emotional instability in the past or present to contra-indicate telling. In the overwhelming majority of those he thought it suitable to tell, the patients maintained their emotional balance and did not regret being told. In some patients it was suspected that they would be upset initially, but later regain composure; and this was largely borne out. Among both those who were told and those who were not, there were equally small groups who never achieved serenity in this last illness. None of the patients in this group, told with care, reacted in a dramatic or excessive way on learning that they had incurable cancer. On the contrary, the social worker, who continued visiting the patient and family throughout the illness, was impressed by the improved family relationships among those who had been told. There appeared to be less tension and desperation at the progressive deterioration in health.

This maintenance of contact and care by people who have imparted tidings of fatal illness is most helpful. People cannot take in all such information of emotional importance immediately. They must be given the opportunity to ask again. Indeed the patient with a serious disease may ask the same questions about his condition again and again, while gradually coming to terms with it. Others deny that they have ever been told.[3] There would seem little kindness in insisting that they realize it if they do not want to hold it in their consciousness. At a later time they may wish to know more. It is a chilling, cruel experience to be told of having an incurable disease and then to be apparently dismissed with no mention of further care, just discarded. Those who confirm a patient's suspicion that he now has little time to live should surely see that he can return to them or some other suitable person who knows of the situation, if he wishes to talk more of the matter. Then he will gain comfort from this honesty.

11 Prolonging Life and Hastening Death

Even when it is clear that a patient has reached the terminal phase of a fatal condition, it is not easy to give up treatments or investigations which have practically no hope of bringing him a further lease of worthwhile life. To what extent should we fight against a seemingly inevitable death? Should a doctor embark on radical measures that may bring discomfort to the last days of many people, because once or twice in his professional life he might have some success? Or should he quietly bring comfort to the dying, perhaps haunted by the thought that he may at some time let an opportunity of cure slip by? And if it is acknowledged that a dying patient's principal need is to be relieved of distress during the last fragment of his life, is there not good reason to consider shortening the period of dying if it only promises to bring much suffering and little pleasure?

PROLONGING LIFE

Any patient will want others to be as keen as himself to gain days of valuable living. The doctor must himself assume final responsibility in some very hard decisions when the end of a patient's chronic, incurable illness is nearing. He may have to decide that the time has come when a repetition of palliative treatments can do no more. The occasion arises, for instance, to stop giving blood transfusions to a hopelessly anaemic patient who used to be restored to reasonable well-being by the transfusions, but then has decreasing benefit from the treatment as the disease progresses.

The hope is that all concerned, patient, relatives, nurses and doctors, have a parallel recognition that this is the appropriate next step. Even though there is to be no further attempt to prolong life, the patient should not feel that he has just been abandoned. He and those who care for him should be in sufficient accord so that, although perhaps apprehensive and sad, there is a mutual but often covert acknowledgement that the time has come. This phase is usually preceded by a time and a pattern of moving towards death. It has been recognized that the patient will die, all have made what adjustments they can, the physical deterioration has accelerated and the last hours have come.[66] An understanding physician once remarked, 'death is almost always preceded by a perfect willingness to die.'[214] The dying person will probably wish others to let him depart in some dignity and not in a welter of failed last measures.

Not all agree on the extent of the measures which should be taken to keep death at bay. Some believe it a duty to preserve every possible fragment of life, others think that an excessive zeal to delay death can make the possible become senseless.[12] An increasing number of vital functions can be maintained by mechanical respirators, artificial kidneys, cardiac stimulators and other ingenious devices. No one will doubt their importance when used for an acutely ill patient, who may thereby survive a crisis and return to reasonable health. Nevertheless, the use of such mechanical aids to prolong a very limited form of life in an incurably ill person remains debatable. If such measures can be continued to bring some useful, enjoyable life, most would wish to use them. If they can only maintain a truncated semblance of life, as in a permanently unconscious being, there is little justification. They can easily cause distress to the living – the fully living.

In view of the problems that may well arise if a person is only just kept alive by a machine, there needs to be considerable thought before initiating their use when there is little hope of future recovery. The decision cannot be left to the patient or relatives, for, among other reasons, they will not be able to judge all the implications of embarking on such measures. If it does turn out that these techniques have only succeeded in maintaining a valueless existence, a burden of suspended dying has been placed upon the patient, if he is conscious, and certainly upon his relatives and friends. This problem of continued care was illustrated by the case of one pleasant, courageous woman who had endured a great deal of illness. She had little remaining healthy lung tissue, but it was necessary to carry out yet one more operation. Her breathing was assisted artifically both during and after the operation, but even so it became apparent within a few days that at times there had not been enough oxygen reaching her brain, which had been irretrievably damaged. Her periods of somewhat confused consciousness, which had initially given rise to some hope of recovery, were over. She was unconscious kept alive by artificial respiration. What should be done? The law has not defined the moment of death, nor has it passed judgement on maintaining artificially such a form of life, but it debars killing.

The ethical problem for the doctor has been discussed from the Roman Catholic point of view by a physician, Laforet.[109] He quotes the comment of Pope Pius XII. Questioned on the use of modern techniques of artificial respiration in unconscious patients with a hopeless outlook, the Pope answered: 'Since these forms of treatment go beyond the ordinary means to which one is bound, it cannot be held that there is an obligation to use them.'[155] Laforet goes on to point out that the physician is fallible and may find difficulty in deciding how 'ordinary' some treatments are. There is also a hesitation to judge the quality of life that remains. It is probably better therefore for the doctor to err on the side of active treatment. It should be possible to ensure that this involves inflicting no undue physical discomfort.

The Church Assembly Board for Social Responsibility has published a helpful booklet on the same problem.[39] The doctor must make such decision about maintaining life in the light of the patient's Christian preparedness for death, and on other factors, such as the patient's medical condition and prospects, his own wishes and beliefs, not leaving out of consideration the views of his kindred and the wider interests of society. It breaks no unalterable Christian law, if, on the principle of loving his neighbour as himself, a doctor allows a person to die. He can comply with God's will that a patient die. Each case has to be judged on its own merits; when the occasion arises, the doctor will need to make his own decision, answerable to society, to his conscience and to God. Most doctors, faced with the problems raised by the unconscious, doomed patient, kept alive by mechanical devices, almost hope for an intercurrent infection that will end the prolonged existence. This is what happened to the woman just mentioned, who could never regain consciousness, and yet her body was not wholly dead as long as the artificial respiration was maintained. To terminate such a life by stopping the ordinary care and nutrition would not seem right and would ask the impossible from nurses. It is an awesome step just to stop the machine, but there is a growing opinion that, when there is clear evidence that the brain will never recover sufficiently to allow consciousness, then the person should be recognized to have died.[23]

Fortunately, as the vast majority of people near death, there is a minimum of doubt and debate over which measures are warranted in attempts to prolong life. The fatal condition alone dictates how much longer a person will live. Increasing medical ingenuity in maintaining life, emphasized by transplantations of hearts from people who have just died, warns us that aspects of the problem are liable to further change. Society will need to re-examine and perhaps pronounce on the disturbing ethical issues of prolonging life, deciding the moment of death and letting people die.

HASTENING DEATH

If it is permissible to allow mortally ill people to die, one cannot help questioning why it should be necessary to wait for the disease to kill them if their remaining life is to contain much physical or mental suffering. Could not euthanasia, in its current sense of bringing about an easy death, be available for those who wish their remaining troubled fragment of life to be brought to an end? The Euthanasia Society, founded in 1935, hopes to encourage public opinion and promote legislation for voluntary euthanasia. They

have no difficulty in finding examples of people who have suffered
a good deal in their terminal illness and most doctors could add
further distressing cases.[50]

Are there good reasons to deny patients the right to end their
lives if they come to a firm and reasonable decision that this would
be best? In this country, since the Suicide Act of 1961, it is not
illegal to attempt to commit suicide, although it is forbidden to aid
another's suicide. Should we not respect rather than interfere
with the wishes of people who have deliberately decided to cut
short their remaining life of illness?[185] Could we not even alter
the law so that in these circumstances a patient could be assisted
in his suicide?[212] Euthanasia could be made legal with some
necessary precautions, perhaps an application by the patient, a
recommendation by his doctor and an authorization from an
appointed referee. To some dying people euthanasia could bring
urgently needed relief, and apart from the minority who view
suffering as an essential path to the attainment of religious merit
or greater nobility of soul, few would dispute that the apparently
useless distress liable to occur during fatal illness ought to be
relieved. In fact, many doctors do not regard the preservation of
life as their primary aim, but more that they should relieve suffering
with all possible skill and devotion. If, in practice, this cannot be
accomplished owing to incurable disease, then, in some eyes, the
necessity to relieve distress in the dying overrides the need to
preserve the remaining life. One study in the United States has
reported that many physicians had heard requests from families
and patients to permit or hasten death's coming.[26] About a third
of these doctors favoured changes in medical practice, but other
surveys have tended to show fewer doctors willing to consider
euthanasia.

Certainly there are some powerful arguments in favour of
allowing voluntary euthanasia as an end to suffering, but many
will not countenance stopping distress by means of deliberately
ending the sufferer's life. Religious beliefs utterly prevent some
people from killing another person or assisting another to kill
himself. Not everyone, however, feels absolutely bound by a
dogma that forbids killings in all circumstances, especially as they

see in the world about them life too often being taken for reasons that are hard to justify. Some doctors have this point of view, but others have, besides their personal scruples against killing, an implicit belief that their own calling prevents them from deliberately destroying life. It need not stop them relieving suffering by effective measures which may carry some risk of shortening a patient's life, but ethically speaking, this appears a very different matter from intentional killing.[109]

Bills to legalize euthanasia have been put forward in the House of Lords in 1936 and 1969.[157] They were defeated although they gained considerable support. Some rejected the idea as incompatible with their Christian belief, but others with religious sincerity do not totally oppose the concept of voluntary euthanasia. There have always been manifest difficulties in devising sufficient safeguards which would not prove too cumbersome. The bedside of each dying man who can no longer bear life is hardly the place for an uneasy admixture of legal and compassionate dispute. Attempts to make simple rules to state when euthanasia is permissible usually have resulted in ambiguous or inadequate guidance.

The thought of selecting people suitable for euthanasia is awesome. There will always be the knowledge that there can be a mistake in diagnosis, even in those who seem near to death. Then there is the question of assessing at what stage of an incurable illness it would be reasonable to end a life. How much suffering must a person face before he is allowed to have his life curtailed? How near death should he be before euthanasia is permissible? There are many people with severe chronic ill-health who must lead very restricted lives with no prospect of improvement. Should their lives be ended? If so, what about other burdensome lives that people endure, unhappy to themselves and seemingly useless or positively troublesome to others? There are also unfortunate people with progressive paralyses making them increasingly helpless. They become unable to feed themselves, to change their own positions or to keep themselves clean; they are imprisoned in their own bodies. They may have little physical pain and it may be difficult to define their suffering. Is voluntary euthanasia permissible for them; and if so, how prematurely may they die?[110]

The problems involved in deciding who is suitable for euthanasia are complex and profound. They are also potentially dangerous. It is important to our ethical code that we do not end human life. In some circumstances it may appear reasonable to make an exception to this policy and permit the killing of a person. It is impossible to define by logical argument the exact circumstances when taking life is permissible and when forbidden. It becomes a matter for judgement, therefore, and judgements can vary, and relevant opinions change for reasons peripheral to the consideration of euthanasia. Hence the value of a dogmatic prohibition of killing; it acts as a bulwark against erosion of our value of other men's lives. We cannot free ourselves of the horrifying memory of events in Nazi Germany where it was accounted permissible to end the lives of those with allegedly incurable mental illness. The culmination of these loosening values of human life in mass murder of people judged inferior prevents many from wishing to make euthanasia legal.[14]

We trust, in our conceit, that our own society could never hold life so cheap, perhaps overlooking or explaining away some of our own historic record. Maybe it would not, but it is not unreasonable to fear that some individuals, some doctors, might become careless with their administration of euthanasia. They might be misguided by a pity that overwhelms judgement. They might blur the distinction between a life that brings too much suffering to the patient and an illness that makes his friends and relatives suffer. There are also unstable individuals, including doctors, whose judgement might be unsound because of the influence of feelings they themselves were unaware of, or unable to control. Certainly it would be unwise for one man to be both judge and executioner.

It is said that the danger of misguided recommendations for euthanasia would not arise as long as the requests to have life terminated were only considered if they originated from the patient. At first sight it may seem a complete safeguard. Nevertheless, a patient's own request for euthanasia could not always be regarded as a valid application, a safeguard against abuse. He would need to be in a sound state of mind to be fit to come to a reasonable and steady judgement that his life should be ended. A person who is very distressed by his terminal illness is in no ideal state to make that judgement. Admittedly, if this point is carried to an extreme it reaches the impasse of asserting that when someone is so distressed as to want death, he is in no mental condition to have his request for euthanasia taken seriously; and, conversely, when a person is so well-adjusted to life that his request to die would be respected, he is unlikely to ask for death. Although this extreme argument may border on the ridiculous, it must not be forgotten that many people when depressed or worn down by suffering may hold just for a while the sincere desire to die. Even fatally ill people who have attempted suicide or requested euthanasia often change their views when their suffering has been relieved or when they have come to terms with the situation which made them so unhappy.[84]

Another cause for a person to ask for euthanasia, for reasons not wholly acceptable, would be when a dying person felt this to be expected of him, because he was a burden upon others. A person with such an altruistic motive is unlikely to disclose this reason when he applies for euthanasia. It is no new thing for people to end their lives or have their lives ended when they appear useless to the community,[182] but in our present standard of civilization this should be an unnecessary, and could be a dangerous, reason for legalizing euthanasia. If euthanasia were accepted, would there be just as great an impetus to improve further the care of the dying? There is a worrying thought that deficiencies in providing care for the incurable could find a latent counter-balance in increased requests for euthanasia.

There are, it appears, many reasons why euthanasia is intrinsically undesirable or so fraught with difficulties of application that it is almost impracticable. Whenever this problem is considered there always lingers in the mind the thought that euthanasia should so rarely be necessary. The suffering during fatal illness ought to be better relieved. But while the dying do sometimes experience anguish, even if in theory it could have been alleviated, the fact that euthanasia could have curtailed much distress for some people

cannot be entirely dismissed. As long as one can truly say that
for the patient merciful death has been too long in coming, there
is some justification for euthanasia. It seems a terrible indictment
that the main argument for euthanasia is that many suffer unduly
because there is a lack of preparation and provision for the total
care of the dying.

12 Who Cares for the Dying?

Of the half million or so deaths in England and Wales each year, just over half now take place in hospital – a gradually rising proportion.[87, 36] About one person in three dies at home and the remainder in other institutions and a variety of places. If a dying person can have adequate care in his own home there is much to be said in favour of ending his days there. Facing the finish of mortal life, often apprehensive or sad, it seems unkind to remove him from the familiar comforts of home. He will not want to relinquish the sustaining affection and the degree of independence that are there.

Indecision comes when reluctance to leave the family is counterbalanced by the inadequate material care available at home, when both he and his family are aware that they are unable to do enough for him in his illness. Although the dying person may need more medical and nursing care than he can get at home, hospital may be seen as a threatening imposition of an apparently unnecessary régime. Going into hospital with little hope of coming out alive means that, alongside freedom, some remaining life is taken away. It is a bit of dying; some things will be left for always. The familiar life is over; the presence of loved people will now be rationed. Even if there is no human company to leave at home, the heart-break and anxiety at leaving a pet who has been life's sole remaining companion should not be underestimated. The understanding doctor will not take lightly the decision to advise his patient to go to hospital to die; the emotional needs should not be unnecessarily subordinated to the requirements of physical care.

If the only available hospital bed is in a poorly staffed and ill-equipped hospital or some inferior institution, there must needs be a compelling reason for a dying person to leave his home.

CARE AT HOME

Most people express a preference to die at home. This general impression has been confirmed by means of systematic studies both of the opinions of patients dying of cancer in hospital[166] and the relatives' reports of the views of those who were cared for at home.[2] This approval could be qualified if these seriously ill people were uncertain whether their family could look after them. Do the dying usually get adequate care if they stay at home? It is said that people nowadays shrug off the responsibility for looking after their very ill relatives. Undoubtedly it is less common for there to be the close ties which come about when three generations of a family live together in the same household. With the increasing trend for young adults to move farther away and make separate homes for themselves and their own children, the family unity is lessened.[216] Hence the older generation, when they fall ill, have become more isolated from their family.

It is easy to find examples of unwillingness or even outright refusal to care for the sick. This is no new phenomenon special to modern society; there have always been children who want to have little to do with their elderly parents and there have always been parents who deserve little gratitude from their children, although their charity would not come amiss. Even if the trend is more towards people dying in hospitals, this can be for the positive reason that there is now more treatment available in hospital, besides the negative reason of personal selfishness in those at home. There is also the practical point that now it is less common to find an unmarried unoccupied woman in the household who can nurse a relative in a suitable room in the home.

In fact, a great deal of devoted care is still given by families to their dying folk. Elderly patients recorded as having died in hospital have often been looked after at home for long periods before admission to hospital, in spite of being, perhaps, immobile,

incontinent and showing mental incapacity.[91] Unreasonable
refusal by relatives to care for people nearing the end of their
lives is unusual; two recent surveys rated this as a cause for
hospital care in only about one per cent of cases.[123, 90] This sup-
ports the results of some previous surveys of medical needs or
of sociological aspects of family life. Sheldon's important study of
elderly people in Wolverhampton and some of Townsend's
investigations give heart-warming examples of love and inspired
kindness, even if they are set in a background of otherwise
frighteningly inadequate impersonal care.[179, 199, 201]

The situation is usually a little easier when a male member of
the family is being nursed at home. As Sheldon found among the
elderly, if the man is ill he could be cared for at home in 80 per cent
of cases, but if the woman fell ill only 64 per cent could be managed
at home. Nursing usually falls to the wife when the man is ill and
the daughter when the woman is sick. Nevertheless, a man can
often rise to the occasion and undertake successfully and for a
long period of time the nursing of his seriously ill wife. They both
prefer the imperfections of this care to separation. If the ill person
had to go to a hospital to die, there would be great distress and
guilt over the failure to carry out this labour of love.

Home care of the dying does impose a strain and if the needs of
the patient outstrip the help available he will suffer and so will
those who attempt to look after him. Many of the surveys of the
care given to those remaining at home with an incurable illness cite
pitiful examples of inadequate facilities. The nursing frequently
falls upon an elderly person, often with frail health, yet faced with
nursing a spouse who will never return home if once admitted to
hospital. She faces the fatigue and the sorrow of carrying out all
the personal care of someone who had been independent and is
now very sick, perhaps helplessly confined to bed for a long time.
She faces tiring and often unfamiliar tasks such as washing the
patient in an inconvenient bed in an awkward bedroom; she may
need to help him use a bed-pan or bottle; she may have to lift an
invalid about the bed when she has neither the strength nor
dexterity to do it. Sheldon found that some elderly women
described the care of a mortally ill person as the most trying time

of their lives.[179] The assistance of a nurse coming to the home does not always provide the anticipated solution, because the dying person may demand that his care come only from his wife. Sometimes an invalid does not appreciate the strain that this nursing imposes and continues to demand more attention and is positively unhelpful during nursing manoeuvres; but sometimes he is only too well aware of the burden he imposes and this knowledge worsens his plight. If, in addition to the strain of nursing throughout the day, the patient is restless and wanders confusedly at night, few can cope for long without help.

If relatives are determined to care for a dying person at home, they will usually find a way of doing this in spite of any lack of amenities, but sometimes the circumstances are shocking. There is still a significant proportion of homes with inadequate water supply for the household, with no bath, with outdoor sanitation or with lavatories shared by too many people and so on.[36] Dying patients are cared for in these surroundings. Whatever their general state and the particular symptoms of their increasing illness, it may be necessary for them either to share a bedroom or to have the living-room as their sick-room with privacy only during the night. Thomson visited the aged sick in Birmingham and found so much hardship in a setting of squalor that he was shocked.[196] He did not think it possible that in post-war England life could be so grim and sordid. He quoted some tragic examples of cases that he had come across only too frequently. One man in the last stages of heart failure slept in the only downstairs room on two chairs. Upstairs there was one room and an attic, and in this house with no bath, no hot water, with shared outside sanitation, lived this dying man, a married couple and five children. Another old lady with partial bowel obstruction lived in an equally primitive slum dwelling and had to share a bedroom with her daughter, son-in-law and a girl of six.

Most homes, of course, are not like this; also, there are sources of help for the sick at home. Under the National Health Service the Local Authorities are obliged to provide certain facilities and may provide some other services. Local Authorities must provide nursing care at home for those who require it and health visitors to advise on the care of ill persons at home. Other services which may be provided by the Local Authorities, sometimes in conjunction with other services and voluntary bodies, including domestic help, delivery of meals to people at home and special laundry services for the bed-linen – the requirements in terms of sheets, blankets and night-clothes for a very sick bed-bound person may be much more than the household can manage and the soiing too great for normal laundry services. The Department of Social Security can grant special financial allowances in certain circumstances. In some areas night nurses or night attendants may be available. It is not very easy to recruit enough people to do this, but some areas in England rely upon part-time workers, even if they can help on only one or two nights weekly.[112]

The social services are distributed very unevenly. Some areas in Britain are well provided for and those caring for the mortally ill patients at home in these areas are fortunate to have every assistance. The district nurses, domestic services and doctors are not asked to do an impossible volume of work and everyone concerned is able to contribute to the full in helping the dying and their families at this sad time. Unfortunately the home care available often falls below a reasonable standard.[94] According to one large survey of the care of patients dying at home with cancer, the general practitioners found the local facilities to be deficient in more than half the areas, rural, urban or industrial.[87] When there are such deficiencies, it explains in part why it has been found that about 15 per cent of people dying at home have a considerable period of suffering.[3, 211] They needed more help than they got; either they should have had more intensive help at home or it should have been possible to admit them to a hospital where they would have had adequate kindly care.

Individuals in the various services may achieve great things, but they cannot be everywhere. Sometimes the services are non-existent, or so sparse and unpredictable that they cannot be relied upon. It is reasonable to cite the information gathered in a fairly recent review of the development of home and welfare services available to old, infirm people, a situation overlapping with the care of those with terminal illness. In spite of some improvements between 1946 and 1960 the Home Nursing services were still numerically insufficient, the health visitors had not increased in numbers, the mobile meal service was still unable to provide meals as frequently as desirable, but there had been some betterment in the domestic help services.[200] Various voluntary organizations, for instance the Red Cross Society, the National Society for Cancer Relief and the Marie Curie Memorial, try to fill some of the needs and have considerable success.

Even where the services are adequate enough to help the dying and their families, often they are not used to their greatest advantage. Not everyone in the full possession of health, wits and pertinacity knows whom to ask or how to ask so that they can extract their requirements from the authorities and organizations set up to provide for them. If those in need of help are frail, bewildered by the responsibility and distress of looking after a loved person who is going to die, perhaps facing the prospect of a lonely future life, and hardly knowing if they are doing right or being a nuisance, it is not surprising that liaison breaks down. They may never get round to asking anyone for help. They may tentatively seek help, but ask it of someone who has little knowledge of the services provided. Or occasionally they may put muddled, impossible requests to an official who gives a negative answer that is justified by the regulations if not by the spirit of the service. If officialdom is faced by peremptory demands for help from a tactless old body, set in his ways and requesting aid in some personally predetermined form not easy to provide, there is likely to be a complete impasse.

Not infrequently, however, neglect comes from the deliberate refusal of the ill person or his family to accept any 'state aid'. They do not wish to ask, because to them it means surrendering their pride and independence. They may even refuse to consult a doctor because they see in this the threat of being sent away from their home to an institution. Often this is an ill-founded mistrust, but not always. Some mortally ill people wish to stay in incredible conditions at home, which, when revealed, place a burden of responsibility on others either to condone apparent neglect or to take steps to alter the situation radically. The dying person often knows in one sense that he ought to be in hospital, but he does not want to go there. To him the coming of the ambulance might just as well be the arrival of the tumbrel.

For the mortally ill at home with families and neighbours to help the situation can be bad enough. Their elderly life-companions may become tired out and their younger relatives may only be able to help if they sacrifice some of their own family life or their paid employment. But for those living in solitude, it can be worse. Of a series of cancer patients being nursed at home, 7 per cent lived alone and thus experienced considerable hardship.[94] Visits by the nurse and doctor meet some needs. Neighbours may help with the housework, preparing meals, shopping, looking after the ill person's interests and often showing great kindness and warm humanity. More distant relatives may come to the aid of the solitary, but often no kin remain or the link is too slight and affection absent. It is not too rare for an isolated invalid to have alienated so many in the past that no one sees good reason to assist now, especially if they anticipate that their offers will be met with abuse rather than thanks.

The care provided for those dying at home is clearly imperfect. Anyone who has been personally concerned in this will be well aware of it. Investigation confirms that patients with malignant disease sent home from hospital may fall victim to administrative muddle, especially when they and their families are asked to cope with the impossible, and no professional person accepts the overall responsibility for providing care.[183] Nevertheless, the rewards of successful home care are great. Although we must be dissatisfied that a proportion suffer unduly in their terminal illness at home, the majority have reasonable care and their families consider that the dying have been adequately tended.[2] Dying persons gain so much by being cared for by an affectionate family; they are better able to maintain themselves as individuals. Remaining at home, not swallowed up in the possible anonymity of the dying hospital patient, they need not doubt they are still part of the family. While among their family, they do not consider themselves as hulks awaiting the end, as long as they can participate, even in a limited role. They can perform household chores, wield a little authority or keep an eye on the grandchildren.

Although incurably ill, they remain a most important part of an extended family, a focal point where younger generations and distant relatives gather, where but for them, much family cohesion would be lost.

If all played their part, most people would be able to die at home if they wished, and the majority do want this. Besides this humane purpose, if further justification were needed, it is more economic to provide the extra help to care for patients at home, rather than the expensive full-time care in hospital. According to one investigation, a small improvement in domiciliary care would make unnecessary a quarter of the applications to admit to hospital the 'chronic sick', many of whom are in their terminal illness.[197] It only needs a little more in the way of nursing and other help.

CARE IN HOSPITALS AND INSTITUTIONS

For various reasons one person in two does not end life at home. Some because their treatment needs can only be met in a hospital; some because the available home care is too scanty; and some because they enter hospital for investigation or treatment and never improve enough to leave. The differing kinds and standards of hospitals in which they die vary as much as do their homes. The range of hospitals includes homes specifically for the dying, hospitals for acute cases, hospitals and institutions for the chronic sick, homes for the aged, and nursing homes.

Some of the homes for the dying are excellent. The familiarity of the staff with death by no means diminishes their individual kindness or the degree of skilled attention they give to people who have little life left. Their morale and devotion is high and their experience enhances their service. Many are affiliated to a religious organization which inspires their vocation, but does not usually impel them to put forward their own beliefs to unwilling ears. Considering their circumstances, patients in well-run homes for the dying are often able to enjoy some of their remaining days in remarkable peace and acceptance. Their worst moments are quite possibly those soon after arrival, especially if they come trusting

in people who have said they were to have a period of convalescence
or new treatment, only to discover that they have been sent to the
hospital to die. In the main, however, the realization that they
actually are dying grows more gently in the company of those
who also face fate with courage. There is often a unity of little jokes
and kindnesses, with gratitude that their discomfort is being
controlled. The relatives and friends who visit them are glad to
see their dignity and comfort restored, when formerly they have
seen them frightened and suffering.

Hospitals and homes for the dying need a high standard of
personal integrity and morale among a staff adequate in numbers
and equipped with enough material facilities, if they are not to
degenerate into awful places. To be admitted to an overcrowded,
poorly maintained ward containing many dying people can be
no kindness to a person who retains all his normal alertness. If
around him he sees gloomy dilapidated buildings, discontented
staff and troubled dying people, he will soon become as aggrieved
as they are. Such hospitals can be improved. Expenditure on
practical design and more attractive décor, making them better
places to be in, can lift the spirits of staff and patients. A link with
another hospital treating recoverable illness may be a help. It will
allow an interchange of ideas and new knowledge, and if any
palliative treatment is needed, this can be carried out in the allied
hospital. The patients appreciate this chance of active care,
knowing that necessary treatments will be given and that no
remedies will go by default. They can more reasonably keep a little
hope and gain comfort thereby.

Many deaths take place in hospitals designed for the care of
acute cases. In these centres is marshalled much scientific apparatus
designed to help in the diagnosis and treatment of remediable
conditions. Sometimes the highly skilled staff are able to rescue
from death people abruptly threatened by various medical or
surgical catastrophes. There is a preference for treating the younger
patient, where all feel rewarded if he is discharged fully fit. There
is also likely to be a disproportionate interest in the rare and the
unusual case. This being so, it implies a covert reluctance to care
for elderly people who are unlikely to recover. They may well

linger awhile in hospital, 'blocking a bed', until they die or are
transferred elsewhere.

The more gentle care necessary for treating dying people may
not be at its best in hospitals catering for acute cases. The traditional design of large wards with a few single or double rooms
does not allow much flexibility in the choice of a suitable bed for
the dying; a sudden transfer of a person with deteriorating health
from a full ward to a lonely side-ward can have bleak implications.
Nevertheless to remain in a large busy ward is not always suitable.
A very sick patient, unconscious or noisy and confused for days,
may upset other people. A fully conscious person in his terminal
illness sometimes may not feel at ease in a large ward because he
just wants the quiet company of his relatives alongside the bed
without their feeling that they are in the way. Besides the material
shortage of suitable wards for the dying in an acute hospital, there
is often not the psychological preparedness to care for them. Some
of the staff are humane and excellent at this, of course, but some
are less good. Owing to their own particular approach to medicine
and their awareness of the acute needs of other curable patients,
they can be half-hearted in seeing to the welfare of the dying.[113]
Although those who die in acute hospitals will have available a
number of palliative or potentially curative treatments and so will
not experience the grosser forms of neglect that other dying people
may suffer, they may feel less important in the eyes of the staff
than they might.

Most people who do not die at home, end their lives in hospitals
or institutions for the chronic sick. In fact, those to be considered
as 'chronically sick' euphemistically include people with fatal
cancers and other conditions.[122] What are the hospitals for the
chronic sick like? They have often been heavily criticized and
sometimes with good reason. Many are outdated public-assistance
institutions taken over as hospitals under the National Health
Service in 1948. In the last few years a great amount of time and
money has been spent on improvements. A start has been made in
adapting the buildings and appointing more staff who have both
interest and training in treating chronically ill, aged or dying
people. More nurses are needed, more physicians interested in

geriatric problems, more social workers, physiotherapists, occupational therapists and so on. Such trained staff can alleviate the physical discomfort of patients with terminal illness and they can hope to make patients' remaining days more than just a period of awaiting death.

In spite of improvement, however, many of these places are quite unsuited to function as modern hospitals. They are often large, cold, damp buildings with no easy access from one part to another, so that it is difficult to get warm meals to the bedside and any equipment into the ward. The absence of lifts means that some patients, once upstairs, stay there until there is the awkward task of getting their bodies down again. Sheldon, visiting and reporting some years ago on some of the old institutions, was moved to use such phrases as 'human warehouses' and 'storage space for patients'.[180] There were large wards with four rows of beds running down their length, cheerless corridors, angled staircases and passages too narrow for wheel chairs. The sanitary arrangements were often appalling, perhaps because when the hospitals were built it was assumed that patients remained in bed, unable to use lavatories. Even this does not explain the deficiencies in sanitation: although bed-pans might be a dominant feature in institutions where patients were expected to be bed-ridden, there were no adequate facilities for cleaning them. Sheldon found hospitals where bed-pans were washed after use in an available lavatory, using a pot of water as there was no immediate supply of running water; they might be washed in the same room as the crockery, and stored in the bath overnight. Bags of dirty linen rested outside the wards at the foot of stairways and spread their smell throughout the building. The nurses battled on heroically. They emerge with far greater credit than we, who are still capable of ignoring the conditions which make muted people suffer. The dissatisfied dead cannot noise abroad the negligence they have experienced.

The deficiencies which occur in the hospital care of dying people contribute indirectly to some of the suffering that takes place at home. The poor reputation of some hospitals, not always still deserved, makes some dying people determined to stay in their own place. Their medical advisers may be reluctant to persuade them to enter hospital if the only hospital vacancies are poor havens. Hence very ill people, requiring almost continuous attention, may still prefer to remain at home, although nurses and doctors cannot spend enough time with them nor arrange for their visits to coincide with the moments when they are most needed. One can have considerable sympathy for unconforming persons like the elderly solitary dying man described by Townsend.[200] He wanted either sufficient help to keep going in his own dwelling or to enter a small home not too far away. He would not accept with complaisance what society had to offer – a chance to end his days as a bed-occupant in a large ill-equipped institution.

Have the smaller homes more to offer? The choice between a good hospital and a satisfactory home where the dying can be cared for must depend upon personal taste or the specific requirements of each patient. A hospital may have a larger selection of special facilities, but these are not often required at the terminal phase. The home may have a personal touch to its rooms, with pleasant surroundings which can bring their own peace. Both types of place can be adequately staffed by kindly, skilled people who inspire liking and trust. But to choose between a below-standard hospital for the chronic sick or a poor home is a painful dilemma. Many dying people or their relatives have to do this, some in ignorance and some with painful awareness of the implications.

In the homes for the aged provided by Local Authorities, some have no special provisions for caring for fatally ill people, even though residents do not have long to live. It is expected that any inmates who become seriously ill will be transferred to the local hospital when necessary. This policy is not wholly approved and some Local Authority Homes have a sick-bay. In the Welfare Homes where people can be cared for during the whole of their remaining life if need be, the elderly can feel reasonably secure that they will not be thrust out into some strange place when their life is about to end. Townsend was impressed by the spirit of the staff in some of these homes.[201] There could be an atmosphere of mutual trust and easy conversation. When a member of the community died, the word was passed round and there was some sense of loss. A few flowers were sent to the funeral and at least one person from the home went to the service.

This may seem little enough, but consider the atmosphere found in some other institutions, often former workhouses partially modernized. They could be about as homely as a traditional barracks, life ordered by rules and prohibiting notices. The staff were often insufficient in number, performing a task with no sense of purpose. Those appointed to staff such institutions, who have to explain away deficiencies and answer criticisms, cannot help becoming identified with the inadequacies that they themselves endure as unchangeable. The residents of some of the homes, as reported in *The Last Refuge*, tended to withdraw into isolation.[201] Developing acquaintanceships did not flourish; they were too soon interrupted by the frequent changes of dormitory or deaths. Life was reduced to an anticipation of the next meal. In such poor homes an old person about to die was often secluded in a room which might come to bear a sinister reputation. If, after his death, other residents asked about his absence, the policy was to evade the question or deny that death had occurred. This furtiveness had its given reason: it was so that residents should not become upset. It might be successful in preventing some momentary expression of grief, but it could mean a lonely, bitter end for the dying person. It could also contribute to a pervasive atmosphere of forlorn personal unimportance. People in such homes for the elderly would not be unaware that they were likely to end their days in the institution, because a fifth or a quarter of them do die each year. They saw that their own death was likely to be equally undignified and anonymous. Personal pride drained away even further. The staff could say of them that they hardly noticed one another's death, but what other resource had they in such an existence except 'not to care.'

Nursing homes, like other homes and hospitals, reach both heights and depths in their care of the dying. Many nursing homes are well run by devoted proprietors who have had much training and experience. The profits of the home are to a considerable extent used to improve the service they give. In these better

circumstances, the last days of a patient can be a time of relative
comfort and kindliness. The nursing home surroundings are
often more congenial to patients than those of a hospital. Fewer
people are involved and there is an atmosphere of greater intimacy
than that of a larger institution. Formality can be at a minimum
without sacrificing any efficiency in nursing. Some aspects of the
hospital régime which are unhelpful to the individual patient can
be dropped. This may avoid the series of battles that can develop
between staff and elderly patients who refuse certain treatments or
the attempts to impose order. In the atmosphere of personal care,
where most people in the nursing home know how the patient is
faring and recognize his relatives when they visit, the moral
support to the family is considered an integral part of the whole
situation. Small homes can attain very high standards of total
care.

Sub-standard nursing homes, however, like the poorer homes
for the aged, can provide a half-concealed, ill-tended shuffle from
life. Ill and elderly people are often admitted to poorly staffed,
poorly designed nursing homes at a time when the care they need
can just about be managed. There is a covert understanding that
they are to end their days there, but at the time of admission it
seems almost indecent to inquire if the home has the necessary
staff and facilities for tending the very ill and dying. Hence the last
few days of the dying person may be spent out of sight of the others
in some unfrequented corner of the home, perhaps normally used
for some other purpose, such as storing spare furniture. The
isolation, plus the further stretching of limited resources in staff
and equipment, may cause the dying more physical discomfort
and mental distress than there should be, sometimes bordering on
neglect. Nursing homes have to be registered and may be in-
spected, but strictures can be met by vague assurances and little
or no action.[87] If the proprietors of the nursing home are in no
mind or financial position to improve the situation, there is little
that outside authorities can do to enforce better care of their dying
patients.

CAN THE PROBLEMS OF CARE BE SOLVED?

Most people who inspect more than a limited field of terminal care find sad or enraging deficiencies. We are unlikely to find a universally applicable perfect solution to the problems of caring for the dying. Some needs will be met by the undramatic moves of making continued improvements in all the present services, eliminating the grosser failings and raising the standards that are too low. Glaser and Strauss propose that the system needs radical reform so as to keep the best of the existing modes of care in addition to providing new facilities, but all of them having a different, improved organization.[66] Their more immediate recommendations are to improve training in terminal care in nursing and medical schools. At the same time the social and psychological aspects of the care of dying people need open review rather than being kept at a level of personal intuition or covert agreement (or disagreement) among each group of staff concerned. They suggest that organization of terminal care needs to be planned to deal more rationally with individuals likely to follow a course taking them in and out of hospitals. Lastly, they recommend public discussion on the issues of terminal care which cannot be resolved solely by professional groups. Indeed, to organize and finance the far-reaching improvements they propose demands that people do face with wider understanding the problems of the dying and those close to them.

As with the strategy necessary to improve the services, a greater readiness to confront the problems of dying is required for the tactics of individual care. Owing to uncertainty over the course of any individual's terminal illness, and the general reluctance to consider the matter at all, the treatment of the mortally ill often drifts along until some crisis occurs. Then, owing to the lack of forethought, and no preliminary discussion between those concerned, hurried measures are taken. It often means accepting an inferior mode of care of the patient because a more suitable alternative is not immediately available.

If the dying person himself cannot make clear his practicable preference for future care, then someone else must make a balanced judgement for him. Among those who do care for the dying person, be they relative, friend, nurse, priest, social worker, family doctor, hospital doctor and so on, there is usually one person who has sufficient knowledge of the dying individual and his medical condition to assume enough responsibility to plan the best course of care. Of course, the family doctor is usually far and away the best person to advise in this situation. Unfortunately, there is at present still some threat to the position and availability of the personal doctor in Britain; if he is lost to us in the way that he is disappearing fast in the United States, we will lose someone who is well able to minimize the distress of terminal illness.

The good general practitioner who can care for his dying patient at home and continue this personal care in an adequate local hospital, if necessary, is in a very favourable position to do the best for each individual. Few family doctors can now do this; they are not often on the staff of the local hospital. Indeed the communication and mutual understanding between the general hospital and the doctor can be quite poor. Many general practitioners feel frustrated either when they attempt to mobilize local services to help care for the dying person at home, or when they wish to get their patient cared for in hospital. Several failures to obtain help may well discourage future attempts to seek aid from a legitimate source.

There are signs that hospital services, perhaps as a consequence, may be changing in scope to provide more comprehensive care for the patient. The traditional part played by the independent family doctor may diminish further and he may be replaced by groups of doctors working in centres with ancillary staff. Alternatively, he may rely more on other doctors providing an 'on call' service for part of the day or night, or he could even be replaced by hospital services – controversial policies which can engender heated debate. Some hospitals have undertaken continued surveillance of patients whom they have treated for illnesses which were expected to prove fatal. For instance, in Newcastle the hospital doctors kept in touch with and visited a group of women who eventually died with pelvic cancer.[169] They noted that the patients' initial willingness to enter hospital often changed to a reluctance to be re-admitted when they felt the hospital treatment might have little to offer. Two thirds of the patients did die at home in varying degrees of comfort. It was apparent that there were some who could have been made more comfortable if they could have been easily admitted to, perhaps, a small hospital near to their home, one where there could be a sense of informality and friendliness in the wards.

Implicit in such continued contact, unless it is very superficial, is a personal link between the people working in the hospital and the patient at home. The mortally ill person and his family realize that he is not discarded. A study of a group of people with lung cancer shows the beneficial effects which may accrue from this liaison.[11] In this case a social worker from a London hospital, with the general practitioner's approval, kept in touch with the patient and visited the home when necessary. Various problems were studied, the resumption of work, the care at home, the strain on relatives who knew the outcome and so on. When it was possible to make long-term plans, some patients went to terminal care homes. Very often the need for more intensive care in hospital came unexpectedly. The value of the medical social worker's liaison then became apparent. Those in hospital knew of the pressure at home and often re-admitted the patient. If it was decided that another form of care was appropriate, then those at home were reassured, in that they knew that the decision was reached by people who were aware of the whole situation. The confidence inspired by the continued personal links made plans more acceptable to the patient and his family. The maintenance of interest throughout gave great emotional support, very welcome to such troubled people.

This pointer to the possible benefits of an extension of traditionally limited hospital function has been confirmed in deliberate schemes of home care based on hospital departments, like the one at Montefiore Hospital in New York.[166] In such arrangements the patients gain from the flexible operation of a team of various medical and social workers. They are prepared to treat people with terminal illness by arranging transport to the out-patient department or by visiting them at their homes. Minor surgical procedures which relieve symptoms, such as draining accumulations of fluid from the body or giving blood transfusions, are carried out at home if necessary. The enthusiasm and interest shown by the medical team is further reinforced by the echoing spirit of other agencies, nursing services and not least, the patients' families. With the guidance and moral support which the relatives receive, they can take over quite skilled tasks of nursing, a great help to others and to themselves. Perhaps, towards the end, the attention needed by the patient increases so much that it is simpler for him to enter hospital, but the dying person's frequent preference for staying at home has to be taken into account. Although home care is not ideal for all patients – it depends on their own condition and that of their families and households – much can be achieved. One London home giving terminal care has provided an out-patient service, close liaison with general practitioners and nursing visits which have enabled many in-patients to return home for long periods of their last illness. This arrangement has many valuable rewards for all concerned. It has certainly shown that when people take a positive interest in the welfare of the dying, their last days on earth need not be distressful.

Mourning

13   Reactions to Bereavement

After a person has died those who knew and loved him continue to suffer. Even if death has been anticipated for a long time, when it finally comes there is a resurgence of grief. The immediate reactions of the bereaved will not be limited to those of straightforward sorrow. The death may cause some initial numbness and then arouse a great turmoil of emotions leading to wide variations in behaviour in different people.

EMOTIONS FOLLOWING BEREAVEMENT

Grief is, of course, the commonest feeling. Misery and despair may fill the minds of the bereaved, so that life seems empty and all ambition worthless. Apathy inhibits any effort and movements are slow; demeanour and expression reveal the sorrow borne. From time to time they experience waves of yearning for the one who has died, especially if there is any reminder of the loss or others express their condolences. Every so often the grief reaches physical intensity; the chest seems to tighten, the breath comes in sighs and all strength melts. But not all those who grieve are apathetic. Some show restless ill-directed activity, starting on jobs that they rarely complete, sitting down for a moment only to get up and tamper with something else. They do not want to eat, and sleep will not come easily because of the agitation of their minds and bodies.[120][48]

Such grief is often accompanied by self-doubt, painful self-questioning, shame and guilt. The bereaved frequently blame themselves for not having done enough for the deceased, even if they have, in fact, performed wonders of care during the last illness. Although it may be clear that they have made the correct choices when faced with the difficult decisions involved in the care of the dying person, after the death they often question the standards of their own conduct. Should they have got the patient to hospital earlier or insisted upon some different plan of treatment? Should they have taken the dying person from hospital to end his days at home, even though it was patently clear that he could have been looked after adequately only in hospital? In their grief, people are very apt to produce more and more self-recriminations. They feel they could have behaved better towards the dead person while he was alive, shown him more appreciation, affection and so on. It is not uncommon for the bereaved even to accuse themselves of having contributed towards the death by their neglect or by the demands they had made on the deceased.

Occasionally such feelings of guilt become so severe as to reach delusional intensity. The self-blame is expressed with such vehement belief and consistency that the bereaved need psychiatric care lest they harm themselves. Suicidal thoughts are far from rare following bereavement and, not infrequently, suicide does take place. Guilt is not the only motive for the bereaved to kill themselves. Quite a few people, having lost someone very dear to them, are convinced that life holds no more. They proceed to an apparently logical conclusion and end their own lives. Usually it is their depressed mood that has hidden from them the fact that life could prove enjoyable again when grief had passed. Occasionally it must be admitted that some face a very bleak and lonely life after a tragic bereavement.

Alongside the mourners' grief and self-criticism may come criticism and blame of others. In our society we are less ready to show such anger or accept that it has any place in mourning. It is recognized as a natural feeling by some primitive communities. The reaction to the death of a member of a tribe may be that the whole community becomes exasperated and enraged.[128] Being deprived by death of a companion can lead to the bereaved tribesman demanding or taking another's life to atone for the loss which has affected his own family, even though the death may have been due to natural causes.[67]

Although the outward display may be less, in Western civilization the bereaved also experience anger and resentment. The picture of mourning found by Lindemann in a series of bereaved people, many of whom had lost relatives in a disastrous night-club fire, was of a distress that often included hostile feelings. It was a relief to these people to be able to express such feelings and to learn that it was neither uncommon nor uniquely wicked to have such angry thoughts.[120] In a study of a number of bereaved people who required psychiatric treatment, Parkes found that a quarter showed considerable animosity towards such people as the doctor or clergy.[151] Doctors are far from perfect and on occasions patients and their relatives have reason to be annoyed with them, but such anger quite often rises up when there is no apparent justification. The bereaved may make wild accusations that there has been neglect or reprehensible failure to diagnose a fatal disease until it is too late. It is a displaced anger, with the doctor providing a not altogether inappropriate target in so far as he has failed to prevent the death. The displacement is more obvious when the priest is a target for criticism and the bereaved may even denounce God. Rather than turn to God when a loved one dies, a few turn away from him for if God can permit such a death to occur he will no longer be their God. The frequent sense of injustice felt by young widows has been described by Marris in his sympathetic account of their reactions to their husbands' death.[127] Parkes has also found that most widows experiencing apparently normal reactions to bereavement had periods of irritability and bitterness, tending to blame others.[152]

The bereaved occasionally add to the burden of other mourners by thinking ill of them. A depressed widower spoke of his feelings about his daughter.

Her mother was having treatment in hospital and she moved her out. She took her away to her home in T'm. I as good as accused her of killing her. She actually murdered her mother; I kept telling her the doctors were not as good in T'm.

In a similar way parents, whose married child has died, may feel or even assert that the son- or daughter-in-law did not show sufficient care. Other relatives may be accused of not helping enough during the last illness, even if the accuser had, in fact, rejected their proffered aid. The good intentions of those who attempt to console the bereaved may be met by angry remarks that they neither understand nor care enough. Funerals have often marked the onset of family schisms.

This floating anger of the mourner may even be centred upon the person who has died.[152] In one survey of seriously distressed bereaved people, 8 per cent expressed anger towards the dead person.[151] Occasionally the deceased is openly criticized in an uninhibited way, and if the bereaved person is not visibly distraught as he makes such hostile comments, he may horrify mourners who are thinking of the departed in idealistic terms. More readily acceptable is the mixture of anguish and anger. This was typified by the repeated calls of a mother, who, at the funeral of her beloved adult son, ignored all around her as she demanded of her dead child why he had left her.

In contrast, the bereaved may experience a sense of relief when the death occurs. This may arise from an altruistic feeling that the dying person's life held no promise of anything but suffering. Those who loved him take comfort that the deceased has found peace, even though it means he is lost to them. Those who nursed him during the last illness may have been reaching the limits of their endurance and confess relief that it is over and that they managed to see it through. But there may be a different sort of relief, which is not readily admitted openly soon after the death. The relationship with the deceased person may have brought a great deal of unpleasantness to those who are now bereaved. Their lives together may have been full of bitterness, or undue domination, or some continuous dissatisfaction which could only be ended by a crisis such as the death of one of them. Sometimes the personal relationship has been reasonably good, but life together has entailed the frustration of some desire. One does not have to look far to find a young person looking after a parent for whom he, or usually she, has the greatest regard, although their life together prevents her from joining those of her own age in leading a fuller life. She does not meet the people she longs to see and may fear that the chances of a happy marriage are slipping by. Her grief when bereaved may be tempered with relief, if this release has not come too late.

OTHER REACTIONS TO BEREAVEMENT

The emotions of the bereaved discussed so far may seem quite understandable, especially the grief and anxiety. The sense of relief is often recognized. Some may be disinclined to recognize anger and resentment as appropriate when someone has died, but most people who have explored the emotions of the bereaved discover these more negative feelings. There are, however, many other less frequent psychological reactions to bereavement, either exaggerations of common emotions or reactions of a more neurotic character. That elusive, perhaps non-existent, boundary between normal and neurotic feelings and behaviour is even more difficult to determine in this context than it usually is.

Continued incapacitating grief is the commonest variation of the usual pattern of mourning.[151] There is evidence that the people who at first do not demonstrate their grief may later show this troubled, chronic state.[152] To recognize a state of grief as being unduly prolonged, however, infers that there is a generally accepted length of mourning. In fact the duration of sorrow varies enormously. Usually, the more severe mental pain eases after one or two or perhaps a few more weeks. Most assume that the grief will have largely abated within six months. This is by no means universal. The majority of widows seen by Marris in his investigation were still distressed by their loss a year later.[127] One of Maddison's studies in the U.S.A. and Australia revealed that 20 to 30 per cent of widows were experiencing some psychological or physical ill-health a year after their bereavement, as compared with 7 per cent of women still married.[124] In psychiatric practice and in life in general, it is far from rare to meet people whose depression smoulders on and on after their bereavement, blighting their lives for years.

Another variety of reaction is the exaggeration of the numbness commonly felt immediately after bereavement. Normally this numbness, this apparent failure to realize fully the extent of the loss and grief, may last a few hours or a few days.[152] Some of the bereaved continue about their business for many days or weeks as if the fact had never sunk in. Their friends await the signs of sorrow, which may come eventually or perhaps will never be shown. In unusual circumstances this may become the normal pattern. Too frequent losses in war can blunt the expression or even the feeling of grief. The saturation with sorrow and the bitter necessity to adapt and carry on reduce the intensity of grief over repeated tragedies. Members of active fighting units in the war noted this subsidence of feeling with rather regretful relief. When the first of their number were killed, the gaps among them were painful. As the losses came again and again they were accepted as someone else's turn to be killed, and the spaces in the unit were quickly filled and obliterated.

If grief does lie hidden for a while, it may finally erupt some weeks afterwards or even show itself at a much later but significant occasion, such as the anniversary of the death. The concealed grief may only be revealed at a further perhaps lesser bereavement. Then the grief at the second loss may seem excessive for the immediate situation, but derives its strength from the delayed release of earlier distress. There is tentative evidence that a psychological illness is apt to arise when a person reaches an age which has a significance in connexion with an important bereavement. Emotional crises have been reported, for instance, when someone reaches the age at which a parent died, or even when his child reaches the age at which the individual himself suffered a bereavement.[79] It is certainly quite common for people to be troubled by the thought that they will not live beyond the age at which one of their parents died.

An insidious effect of bereavement is the long-term change that the loss of a parent may have on children. Young children often show an ability to subdue quickly their grief over losses – or perhaps it just ceases to be obvious – but this may be at the cost of consciously or unconsciously denying their need for the affection which has been taken from them.[20] It may seriously impair the normal development of their personality. In the last few years more evidence of the long-term legacy of such childhood loss has been collected; but which of the many emotional and material changes in the lives of bereaved children warps most their future development is hard to say. Children who have lost a parent do show when they grow up a greater liability to depression, to sociopathic behaviour or to obvious self-damaging acts such as suicidal attempts.[25, 71]

Some of the more immediate responses to bereavement gradually shade into neurotic forms of emotional distress. In this situation occasional feelings of panic occur in so many people that it may be considered a normal reaction.[152] Other illogical fears may arise, such as the phobias of being alone, or of being in an enclosed space, or fears of dirt, or, more immediately relevant, undue fears of death or dying. Bereavement may mark the onset of a troubling sensation called depersonalization, with a sense of inexplicable self-change, of unfamiliarity or unreality.[167] In some ways this sense of altered feelings is self-protective, as if it avoided the full impact of painful grief. The bereaved may also experience obsessional ruminations, recurrent thoughts which cannot be put out of the mind, although the sufferer tries to do so. This has a similarity to the common inescapable preoccupation with the deceased; as, for example, in a woman whose husband had died unexpectedly from a heart attack. Many months later she would still repeatedly go over in her mind every detail of his death. Other less closely relevant obsessions and recognizably unreasonable thoughts may plague the mind of the bereaved. One woman, following a death in the family, could not rid herself of the thought that her own breathing might stop. Another woman had sacrilegious thoughts repeatedly intruding into her prayers. A man, following the death of his father, was beset by the recurrent thought that he might impulsively attack his wife.

Although emotional disturbances usually predominate in the bereaved, it is quite common for changes of physical health to accompany or even overshadow the troubled feelings. Bodily symptoms of fatigue, insomnia, loss of appetite, loss of weight, and so on, may be part of any marked depression of mood. Some of the bereaved complain little of their grief and are more aware of the physical symptoms of headache, breathlessness palpitations, blurred vision, exhaustion, sleeplessness, and so forth.[40, 124] In a study of the disturbances of health experienced by widows, it was shown that they needed to consult their general practitioners much more often than usual during the first six months of their widowhood, both for physical and psychological symptoms.[150] They required much more in the way of sedative drugs during the eighteen months after their bereavement – an indication that the disturbance of function was not short-lived. Elderly people who suffer bereavement are especially likely to experience their distress as predominantly physical.[191] A few who suffer the stress of losing someone dear to them may experience not just the bodily symptoms that accompany depression but develop a psychosomatic disease. Ulcerative colitis, asthma and other conditions have come on following a bereavement. [121, 131]

It is known that widows and widowers for some while after the death of their spouse run a greater risk of dying than married people of similar age. One survey in Wales reported a tenfold increase in mortality amongst men and women in the year after the death of their wife or husband.[161] Other investigations have recorded smaller but significantly increased risks. In England it is more apparent in widowers, who have as much as a forty per cent increase in mortality rate in the first six months after bereavement.[217] This is not accounted for by such explanations as both the deceased and the temporary survivor dying from the same cause. The rise in mortality rate is due to a number of conditions, in some of which self-neglect could play a part. The increase in suicide among the bereaved contributes its quota. There is a tendency for widowers to die more frequently than expected from cardiac disease – 'broken heart' – or a similar illness to the wife.[153] The rise in mortality among widows is less than in widowers. One study carried out in England showed the slight increase to be mainly in the second year of widowhood.[42] A report from North America revealed a more noticeable rise in the number of deaths following the demise of wife or of husband, especially among the younger people up to the mid-thirties. For widows the mortality rate rose to twice the normal for married women, and for widowers of this age there was a fourfold increase at one stage after their wives' death.[105]

THE CAUSES OF SEVERE BEREAVEMENT REACTION

Clearly bodily discomfort amounting to serious physical ill-health, and mental distress culminating in well-recognized psychiatric disorders, can be caused by bereavement;[149] can we predict who is likely to react more severely to this stress? We know something, if not a great deal, about which of the bereaved tend to suffer most, which sorts of death are liable to bring them greater anguish, and which personalities are most vulnerable.

Severe bereavement reactions occur more often in women. In various published series of patients needing psychiatric treatment following a bereavement, younger and middle-aged widows appear more frequently than other relatives; losing a husband can so utterly disrupt emotional and social balance. If, in addition, the widow sees those about her during her bereavement as unhelpful and unsympathetic, whatever the cause may be, she is less likely to recover well from the crisis.[125] The loss of a child will also bring great anguish to a woman.[120, 215] Moreover, the mental disturbances that occur in those ill-prepared to withstand the untimely death of a child may be slow in responding to treatment.[116] This is especially so if the mother had centred many of her unfulfilled hopes upon the child, living vicariously through her child's existence and the anticipation of the child's future.[144]

Greater shock and mental disturbance follow the unexpected death. Although the foreknowledge that a loved person will soon die does not eliminate the eventual distress, a more gradual sorrow and anticipatory mourning can help the grief when death does come.[36] In the study of the dying children, already referred to in a previous chapter, the length of the fatal illness influenced the reactions of others to the death of these youngsters.[140] The doctors and nursing staff came to know the mothers well. They saw that when the mothers had carried with them for four months or longer the knowledge that their children were fatally ill, they came to have a greater acceptance of the child's death by the time it came near and finally took place.[104] In contrast, incidentally, members of the hospital staff were more troubled when children whom they had treated for a fatal illness for a long time eventually died. For them, the time interval had increased their affection for these young patients.

The unexpected death from suicide brings great distress to the bereaved. Besides its tragic, shocking quality, it leaves others with a greater sense of failure than that which follows a natural death. There may well be some justification in the thought that the death could have been prevented or that the bereaved had some responsibility for it. Suicide carries an implied accusation of not caring enough for the one who has ended his own life. Occasionally the comments or the notes of the suicidal subject make the accusation explicit and cause further anguish.[190]

Some personalities are predisposed to break down on experiencing a stress such as bereavement. This is especially so in people with complex, inconsistent emotional feelings towards the deceased – and people of unstable personalities are apt to form such relationships. If they have been shy, timid folk who are left without emotional support when the person on whom they rely has died, this increases their liability to collapse.[148] People who habitually convey the impression of being immature seem to be less able to bear the stress of bereavement.[215] Although it might be anticipated that neurotic people would easily be overwhelmed by the added stress of another's death, they are not particularly vulnerable; those who have suffered a depressive illness in the past are, however, prone to break down again.[120] It must be admitted, nevertheless, that personality alone does not allow us to anticipate how distressed or mentally disturbed people will be when they are bereaved; it is the nature of their relationship with the deceased which appears to be more significant.

PSYCHIATRIC HELP FOR THE BEREAVED

Helped by others who show a sympathy for their sorrow and a tolerant understanding of any occasional discordant emotion, most people endure their grief until it comes to its natural end. Occasionally the mental disturbance consequent upon bereavement may be so severe that it goes beyond the point where other friends and relatives can give sufficient comfort. What medical treatment is there for the bereaved who become psychologically ill? Various drugs can ease their anxiety, lighten depression, relieve insomnia and so on. Hospital care may be necessary if their disturbed mental state prevents them from caring adequately for themselves, especially if there is a likelihood of their attempting suicide. Often, psychotherapy can help the bereaved in their endeavours to adjust to the severe loss. It may have more to offer than drugs or electro-shock treatment, although this is not always the case.[120, 6]

The frequent failure of physical methods to give lasting relief to those who mourn is understandable. We cannot expect and perhaps should not desire to render people quite tranquil or impassive when human relationships are broken. Psychotherapy often aims to help patients attain a greater awareness of the nature and roots of their own grief; the self-understanding often brings relief. Bereaved people will not be able, nor want, to root out all tender feelings and links with the dead; but they can preserve memories or maintain a feeling of spiritual contact with the deceased in ways that are not distressing or disabling to future life. With help and with time they should come to view the turmoil of feelings about the dead person in better perspective, accepting that for a while they must bear the pain of the loss.

The bereaved are often helped by this sympathetic understanding of their fear and guilt. They are reassured to know that they are not the only ones to experience such feelings as anger, or the dread of losing their sanity, or the sense of losing all affection for those they normally love. It may be a little while before they can believe again that emotional life has not been irrevocably emptied, and that they can learn new patterns of living. For instance a very depressed man was admitted to hospital a few months after his wife's tragic death. She had been depressed for some time and finally left the house. After a dreadful period of waiting she was discovered to have taken her own life. This widower felt lost without her, he was often in tears and wondered if he should end his life too. He saw little hope for the future and suspected that some people blamed him for his wife's death. In hospital he found he could speak freely to the doctor about his feelings. His grief soon ceased to be as overwhelming. He began to plan again for the future and soon felt able to take up the threads of life again. People often are helped by a few psychotherapeutic interviews over a period of four to six weeks.[120]

Psychotherapy for the bereaved means more than a doctor showing sympathy and kindness towards patients. It implies that the therapist has a conception of the way that instinctive forces have produced the state of mind that is distressing; it also implies that he believes that he can help patients achieve a more comfortable integration of their conflicting feelings and motives. The concepts used in psychotherapy are often derived from psychoanalytic schools. Although some of the ideas involved have their scientific imperfections, they play a useful part in psychological treatment. They also provide some explanation of the mental phenomena experienced by bereaved people.

One mechanism of the mind which is well recognized is that the mind seems able to deny the very existence of something that is too overwhelming. It is quite normal for bereaved people to be initially unable to grasp the fact that a person they loved has died. Apparently refusing to credit what they have been told, or even witnessed, they may carry on automatically in a somewhat numbed fashion for several hours as if the death had not occurred. All knowledge of the disastrous loss which can alter irretrievably their manner of life is temporarily suppressed or repressed. Subsequently there follows the intellectual admission that the death has occurred. Occasionally this denial reaches abnormal proportions; an individual may continue to insist in spite of all evidence to the contrary that the death has never taken place. One man whose marriage had been a mixture of mutual support

against the world but antagonism within their partnership, was
shocked by his wife's sudden death while they were separated.
For months he was depressed and bitter, sometimes mourning
her loss. But quite often he insisted that she had not died, defying
the evidence of his daughter's statements, photographs of the
grave and so on. By helping him come to terms with the emotions
aroused by his wife's death, he was also helped to acknowledge
that she had died.

Even though the logical mind sooner or later accepts the loss,
the emotional acceptance may prove harder to achieve. With
such mental ferment, perceptions can be distorted. The unconscious hope or the extreme desire for the loved person still to be
alive may be conducive to hallucinations of his presence. It is a
dramatic but quite common event for the bereaved to have the
experience of apparently seeing or hearing the dead person.
Quite normal people, grieving over their loss, have glimpses of
the person who has died. They may hear the familiar voice,
perhaps saying their name, or recognize the footsteps or customary
noises about the house. Usually it is soon realized that this is a
trick of the senses, but the experience is often extraordinarily
vivid and apparently real. People having such hallucinations may
wonder if they are going mad, but it usually comforts them to
know that many other sane people have similar experiences
following bereavement. In fact, a recent inquiry by a general
practitioner in Wales revealed that about one out of every eight
widows or widowers in his practice had hallucinations of hearing
the dead speak, and a similar proportion claimed to have seen the
deceased.[160]

Another psychological mechanism, which often appears to
make the loss of a loved person more bearable, is that which
creates the continued sensation of his presence. Some bereaved
people deliberately cultivate this sense of presence, communing
mentally with the one who has, in fact, died. The widows whom
Marris interviewed at home spoke of the feeling that their husbands
were still present, and about half of one series of bereaved psychiatric patients had a similar impression.[127, 147] Many of the people
known and interviewed by Dewi Rees in Wales said that this sort

of experience could continue for years, and that they found the feeling of continued presence of their deceased wife or husband helped them.[160] Indeed, such hallucinatory experiences were reported more frequently by people who had been happily married. Occasionally this is not a comforting sensation. When the home seems charged with the presence of the dead person it may become unbearable, and people often feel that they must escape, if only for a moment. They may even have to leave the house for good. There are bound to be haunting memories of life together. The bereaved often find themselves carrying out actions better suited to the past, perhaps making familiar preparations like setting the table for two people though now they are alone. The incomplete acceptance of the death may lead them, months later, to be subconsciously listening for the accustomed footsteps and sounds of the opening door, for a home-coming which now, they have to painfully remind themselves, cannot be.

Besides these responses of incomplete acceptance of the death, which can be looked upon as, on the whole, short-term compensating mechanisms, there are other mental processes evolving towards the further adjustment, or occasionally maladjustment, of the bereaved. Normally, changes within the personality seem to bring some compensation for the actual loss. This is a field of psychology that has been intensively studied by psychoanalysts. The brief comments made here cannot do justice to their concepts, which are described more fully in other writings. It is a part of psychoanalytic theory – and, indeed, of many concepts of man's relationship with fellow man – that people identify themselves to a variable extent with those close to them. The psychoanalyst is particularly concerned with the way that one individual incorporates into his own personality the practices, attitudes and feelings of another. When a close emotional bond is broken by death, it is held that the bereaved compensate for this loss by further incorporating and preserving elements of the character of the deceased in their own self. This manoeuvre to maintain features of the deceased's personality can, to some extent, be carried out with conscious deliberation. The bereaved may undertake to fulfil the wishes and the ambitions of the loved one. When encountering difficult problems, they take the solution they believe the dead person would have chosen.

The theory of unconscious identification with the deceased is supported by the examples of those bereaved who begin to have the same disease symptoms as the one who has died, although they do not usually recognize them as such. This is not the same as the hypochondriacal symptoms of those who fear they will die from the same disease. It is illustrated by the case of an elderly Cockney labourer, outwardly cheerful but inwardly a rather lonely man, who would have liked to have had the happiness of a life with more affection rather than the substitute cheerfulness of humorous repartee. He eventually gained a happy relationship with a granddaughter, but she died tragically of an abdominal tumour. He collapsed at her death and then for two years attended doctors as a rather gloomy man with abdominal symptoms. It was only when the full story was obtained that the psychological relationship was noted between the abdominal symptoms that troubled him and the symptoms that his granddaughter suffered; subsequently his symptoms improved. Physical symptoms, newly acquired, are not the only manifest signs that the bereaved is unconsciously incorporating some features of the dead person. It is not hard to find bereaved people who have taken on various mannerisms of the one they mourn, reproducing familiar gestures, the style of dressing or habits of speech.

Such outward signs are gross instances of the subtle intra-personal adjustments that are going on. If the bereaved can achieve a balance by finding within themselves or taking into themselves something of the person they have lost, then recovery from grief can occur. Abraham, who considered the cause of depression of mood from the psychoanalytic viewpoint, developed the theme that most people come to terms with the problem of re-instating a lost loved person in their inner world. Those who fail to manage this continue to mourn and are melancholic.[1] Freud had earlier expounded on the ambivalent nature of the emotional bonds which exist between people who are very close.[6,7] When bereavement comes, the adjustment to the loss is made difficult because neither the love nor the person were perfect. A stable adjustment to another's death involves assimilating both the loved and the hated elements of his personality. As a consequence the bereaved must experience some self-hate, some self-accusation, some guilt. If this is extreme it will cause severe depression. The bereaved who cannot tolerate having felt some dislike for the deceased during his life will consciously or unconsciously accuse themselves of having some desire for his death. In such primitive mechanisms of the mind, the wish for another's death carries blame for that death. The psychotherapist often aims to allow patients to express these painful, primitive ideas that are not easily acknowledged. This often helps bereaved people to achieve a better emotional balance.

The importance attributed by the psychoanalyst to the patterns of reacting that developed in infancy has been emphasized by Melanie Klein in her explanation of the adult's reaction to bereavement.[102] The losses that take place in adult life echo the losses experienced as an infant. The adult who has something of great importance taken from him is apt to react in the same primitive way as the child responded to deprivation. An infant tends to see things as wholly good or wholly bad. If something wholly good is lost – and Melanie Klein emphasizes the loss when breast-feeding is stopped – then the infant has a primitive feeling of guilt. There is self-blame for having bad, aggressive impulses which must have caused the good thing to be taken away. The bereaved tend to regress to this simple reaction of the child. The stable mature person comes to accept that things are rarely wholly good or bad. He tolerates the loss and guilt in bereavement without being overwhelmed by them. Some people, who cannot attain their equilibrium by themselves, can be helped to reach it.

These theories concerning the important psychological processes of those who mourn are founded on detailed descriptions of feelings, often based upon close introspection, and the observation of some aspects of the behaviour of the bereaved. They are concepts that the psychotherapist may utilize in his treatment of depressed bereaved patients. But the intra-psychic events, whatever their explanation, do not pursue their course regardless of current happenings in the world about. Mourning is enacted in society. The bereaved will receive some comfort and help from others. After the loss of a person, new patterns must be established within the family and with friends and in a wider society that expects individuals to show a balance of personal dependence and independence. Mourning cannot be complete unless the bereaved succeed in making an adequate worldly adjustment without the one they have lost.

14   Mourning and Restitution

The pattern of mourning behaviour is strongly influenced by the inner feelings already discussed, but it is also shaped by convention and the immediate duties which have to be carried out after a death. If mourning proceeds normally the emotions and activities of the bereaved will gradually move towards a stable adjustment for the altered future.

MOURNING

There is usually sufficient harmony between the feelings of the bereaved and social practice for people to find the customs of mourning helpful. In the usual circumstances of our society the open expression of strong emotions is largely inhibited. During times of mourning, however, an outward display of grief is regarded sympathetically. Friends may even encourage and join in the shedding of tears. A few of the bereaved, however, would rather that the contagion of others' sorrow and repeated references to the death were not there to increase their own distress. During mourning the instinctive withdrawal from conviviality is fostered, with an expectation that social engagements will be limited. If not dressed in the black of deep mourning, the bereaved are expected to choose sombre garments which reflect their mood. Gay clothes which enhance the appearance would seem disrespectful or adjudged so symptomatic of human vanity as to be callous or near to wickedness. The Jewish mourner maintains the tradition of wearing a rent garment. It parallels the more vigorous damage to self or garments frequently seen in other cultures.

The practice of mourning provides more than this socially approved catharsis of grief. It insists that the death has occurred, repeatedly demonstrating this fact in various ways over a few days so that the bereaved, whatever their state of mind, accept the painful knowledge, assimilate it and can begin to plan accordingly. Viewing the body and taking part in the funeral emphasize beyond all doubt that the person is really dead. The condolences, the discussion of the deceased in the past tense, the newspaper announcements, the public recognition of the death, all affirm the loss.

Any inner thoughts of criticism of the dead, any selfish relief that he has gone, are overshadowed by the manifest respect for the one who has died. There is quite enough grief experienced from the loss to make the loyal demonstration of sorrow quite genuine, and it helps suppress any painful recall of ambivalent sentiments felt for the deceased during his lifetime. It would be in extremely bad taste, almost wicked, to say unkind or critical things of the recently dead. Obituaries are eulogistic and the bereaved may sincerely express warm sentiments and idealized views of the deceased, opinions which can on occasions contrast pathetically or ludicrously with an antipathy that had existed during life. Relationships between the living are rarely perfect, but it is so much easier in the immediate period of mourning to think of the deceased as ideal, to regard the personal separation as nothing but loss, and to feel the dead worthy of all honour and respect. If grief is deep, it may be some while before the deceased can be sincerely mourned for the imperfect person he more truly was.

In Western civilization religious observances for the dead appear to be diminishing. Jung has said that in more sophisticated society the need to do something for the dead has been almost rationalized out of existence.[98] In Britain the panoply of death has been reduced over the last few decades. There is no longer the extensive Victorian ceremonial of black-edged invitation cards, full mourning, velvet-palled coffin, garlanded horses, with a sumptuous repast after the interment. The monuments are not so huge or pretentious; nowadays we are not necessarily filled with respect at the sight of some of the ponderous marble carvings in Westminster Abbey. The taste for ceremonial is less, except when a public figure is mourned. The feeling at the funeral is more one of personal and shared grief rather than heroic sorrow. We could not now sing vigorously some of the Wesleyan funeral hymns.

> Ah, lovely Appearance of Death:
> No Sight upon Earth is so fair.
> Not all the gay Pageants that breathe
> Can with a dead Body compare.
> With solemn delight I survey
> The Corpse when the Spirit is fled,
> In love with the beautiful Clay,
> And long to lie in its stead.

Gorer has inquired into the increasing cultural uncertainty over the manner of expressing grief and the observances of mourning in this country.[70] Not only has the formality of the funeral diminished, but the visits to the house of mourning and the respectful viewing of the body have declined. This change is more apparent in the professional and middle classes. Respects are paid to the body by less than half of those in the higher social classes, but by three quarters of the other classes. Mourning dress is being abandoned; it is more common to make small adaptations or judicious selection of current dress. Fewer people make a formal cancellation of social engagements for a predetermined period. If social activities are curtailed, it is more likely to come directly from withdrawal of interest and changes in personal contacts rather than an announced policy.

If the convention of elaborate rituals of mourning is questioned, it is not surprising that there have been criticisms of the manner and costs of funerals. Some criticisms may be well-deserved, but the funeral director may also become an innocent target for the displaced resentment of the mourners. They may find no satisfaction in the embellishments and the extravagant display of the funeral, and many can ill afford them. It is to be hoped they will meet a funeral director who is perfectly willing to meet their wishes. If, instead, they are over-encouraged to spend lavishly, the bereaved may reluctantly acquiesce in the unwanted expense, or become very angry and bitter at being put in a position of appearing parsimonious in respect of the person they loved.

Those who have read *The Loved One* by Evelyn Waugh are unlikely to forget his satirical portrayal of the American funeral customs.[206] Jessica Mitford gave a disquieting account of the United States funeral trade, geared to extract far too much money from the bereaved.[134] The dazed relative in his grief was very susceptible to blandishments to inter the loved one in a fitting (expensive) manner. This included embalmment, a full cosmetic treatment, specially designed foundation garments and finery to dress the corpse with the fixed social poise of the living, costly elaborate caskets, expensive cemetery space and an average total charge that amounted to well over a thousand dollars. In Britain she found the comparable figure could be a modest fifty pounds, although this would not include elaborate attention to the body, usually thought unnecessary in this country. It is quite possible at the present time to have a socially acceptable funeral for an average sum of about ninety pounds without there being aspersions of disloyal meanness.[209] It is, of course, very easy to spend a great deal more, but in Britain the funeral director is usually both tactful and helpful in this respect. Miss Mitford's account of the recently acquired US funeral traditions shows that in most centres the bereaved would need to be very determined to effect this sort of economy, unless they had had the foresight to belong to one of the funeral societies that plan for the members' funerals at a cost of less than two hundred dollars.

Whatever its other functions, the funeral has to deal with the practical task of disposing of the body. Burial has always been the commonest means of disposal. The material problems of burial in sites set aside for the purpose clearly increase in densely populated areas, where the churchyard can no longer cope and even extensive cemeteries become full. Cremation is becoming increasingly common in England since the formation of the Cremation Society in 1885.[158] The Vatican lifted the ban on cremation in 1964. All methods of disposing of the body try to balance aspects of reverence for the body with practical considerations of hygiene. Not to be forgotten is the lingering uncertainty that life might not be extinct. Extraordinarily detailed precautions against premature burial have taken. During the last century, in one town it was necessary for a cemetery inspector with knowledge of resuscitation to be constantly at hand to be summoned either by the mortuary porter on watch or through the special provisions available to those who might recover after being mistaken for dead. As has been the custom elsewhere, no burial took place until there were early signs of decomposition.[37] Proceedings like this are aroused by primitive fears and wishes rather than practical need.

At the burial site, and occasionally at the time of the disposal of the body, memorials are placed to symbolize the respect of the living and assert their much-needed belief that the dead have not been entirely annihilated. For the spiritual elements and the psychological needs of the mourners often outweigh the material, occasionaly somewhat sordid, aspects of the funeral. At the funeral service religious beliefs on life and death come to the fore. Most religions hold out comfort and hope to the mourners, assuring them that their loved one has embarked upon a better eternal life. The mourner may be given a particular part to play in the continued existence of the dead. We no longer place food and treasure in tombs nor kill animals and slaves at the place of interment, but special prayers are said for the soul that has gone on. In the Roman Catholic religion masses are celebrated for the dead and All Souls' Day is set apart for the commemoration of the departed awaiting in Purgatory. In the Jewish faith regular prayers are prescribed for the first year of bereavement, for the anniversary of a parent's death and for certain holy days. In this way the religious bond is maintained between the living and those who have died. The sense of service and respect for the dead can also be maintained by regular visits to a tended grave or placing In Memoriam notices in the newspapers. Charitable funds are named after the deceased and good works are done in their name so that they will not be forgotten.

RESTITUTION

Mourning has its necessities, but there comes a time when it should be done with. The conventions of mourning, besides giving a guide to acceptable behaviour in grief, may also help the bereaved by indicating when it is time for them to throw off their sombre mood and again participate actively in life. There is an innate wisdom in the evolution of accepted mourning periods such as the three days sometimes accepted by Christians, or the seven days better observed by Jews.[92] In the *shiveh* period for Jews, there is intensive mourning and special prayers for the dead throughout the day. Visitors come to the house, where the chief mourners remain, and speak to them of the deceased, bringing considerable comfort. More normal life is resumed after this week although there are still some mourning observances prescribed. In England, religion does not give to most people such a clear guide to the length of mourning, and the previous social conventions which dictated matters have almost disintegrated. Gorer believes that the current absence of prescribed behaviour in mourning materially increases the chance of maladjustments to bereavement.[70] It would be an oversimplification to regard these as mere cause and effect. Undoubtedly many would now be helped by having well-defined mourning customs to adhere to, and it is common enough in modern society for many to fail to adjust fully to bereavement. But it is not only since the recent decline of outward mourning that grief could be prolonged, or sustained covert sorrow distort a person's life.

Fortunately the large majority of people achieve a sound and lasting restitution of emotional balance. A man who had been grief-stricken for weeks after his wife's death said: 'What's the point of going on? It's just twenty-four hours of pain and you can't get over the fact that I've lost her. People keep on telling me to make a new life, but how can I? There's no future but loneliness and pain.' After some sympathetic help, however, he was soon planning how he could manage his home and was inquiring of a family friend if she would keep house for him. Although mourners have some loyal disinclination to throw off sorrow, they are relieved when grief does ease. As one widow said: 'For a day I was my old self again. It was a relief to be happy again and to know that I had not been totally submerged. It still hurt when it all came back, though.'

The innate resilience of man is fostered by sympathetic and material help from others. Human nature and society is such that the demonstration of sorrow that occurs in bereavement acts as an appeal for help.[15] Condolences to those who grieve are accompanied by offers of help. The bereaved comfort each other. Besides the religious value of the funeral service, the sense of shared occasion and sorrow assists the participants. The social gathering after the funeral is one aspect of mourning in Britain that is still widely observed. Assembled together informally, with something to eat and drink, the mood seems to lift a little. The good qualities of the dead person are discussed in a lighter manner. A little laughter may spring up, and if the majority appear to approve rather than condemn, it may spread. Relatives and friends who have not met for some while renew their acquaintance. Those who have felt very lonely in their loss may be told sincerely and repeatedly that the others wish to visit them and to be visited. There are social links available to the bereaved within the extended family if they wish to take advantage of them.

Nevertheless, it is not easy, and sometimes it is impossible, for the bereaved to replace the sort of affection they have lost. They ancnot transfer to another person the quality of feelings and shared atcivities that had existed with the one they loved. In our particular society, based in the main on small family units, the death of one member of the unit, which may be as small as a couple, has a relatively severe effect on those who are left. Their loss is great and their grief in keeping. The likelihood of finding a suitable substitute is small because the relationships with the deceased were unique; living in small groups engenders close and complex emotional involvement between individuals. In a small family there is only one person for each role. If the mother dies, for instance, there is a loss of a unique person and the one who has done all the mothering. Where family or group life actively involves a much larger number of people, the loss of the true mother still leaves many maternal women, aunts, elder sisters and so on, who have participated in motherly functions in the past. Therefore the loss felt by those who still need mothering is not quite as great.[204]

The woman who loses her husband has, in our society, a considerable readjustment problem – and widows are commoner than widowers and less likely to re-marry.[35] We attribute a special significance to the monogamous matrimonial bond and the widow rarely feels that the same quality of affection could be regained in another marriage. Nor may the other relatives of the deceased whole-heartedly support her if she does plan to re-marry. The children, for instance, may show considerable antagonism to a step-parent. In several polygamous societies it is accepted that the widow and her children automatically become the wife and children of a specified relative of the former husband, usually a brother. At least this ensures that they maintain some niche in the community. In our society the widows who do come to accept the idea of re-marriage may have considerable difficulty in making a suitable match. Rather than endure too great a loneliness or have the problems of bringing up children without a father, some widows embark on make-shift second marriages, often aware that they risk making a mistake which will not be easily rectified. Re-marriage is more likely to take place to someone who has previously been married. Marris visited seventy-two young and middle-aged widows who had lost their husbands on average two years before. Twelve had re-married, nine thought they might, twenty-nine were undecided about marrying again and twenty-one were against it. They often regarded a second marriage as one of convenience and felt that the children would be opposed to their re-marrying. They feared that there would be unfavourable comparisons with the first marriage.[127]

Interviews with some couples who had re-married after being widowed indicated that satisfying second marriages could be obtained. These people in Canada recognized that the problems and the partners on re-marriage required new forms of adjustment; comparisons with the past could be unhelpful. It was quite probable that the second marriage might bring about loosening of the ties with old friends or even relatives. If children were involved, the replacement of a parent had its difficulties but affection and time usually led to success.[177]

Other broken relationships besides those due to the death of a husband or wife may be re-established after a style. Those who have lost a parent, and still need one, often find someone they can regard in that light. With young children, of course, this need is universally recognized. A grandparent may come to act as mother or father, and both young and old benefit from this. Grown-up 'children' may also find some mature person whom they can now turn to for support, perhaps marrying a motherly or fatherly person or coming to regard some suitable soul as an aunt or an uncle. Parents who have lost a child may well wish to replace their loss. They may deliberately conceive another for this purpose, or they even come to regard one of their other children as the sub- stitute for the one who has died. It is not unknown for a child to be re-named after a dead sibling. The emotional atmosphere sur- rounding such stand-in children is unlikely to prosper their developing personality.[29]

Beside the need to replace, when possible, the bonds of affection that have been broken by death, the bereaved may well be in urgent requirement of material and practical help. These worldly needs are apt to become most pressing for widows. Men are more likely to be independent, at least financially. Bereaved adults usually wish to preserve a considerable measure of independence, but for a woman this often means a big drop in the standard of living. Widows with children, unless they have considerable private financial provision, will need either to work and get help in the care of the children, or exist on the borders of poverty.[127] Help is accepted most readily from the family, and best from the widow's own relatives. As described by Marris, it is usually given in the form of minding the children, helping with jobs in the house, presenting useful gifts and passing on articles of wear and so on. The widows may well receive slightly camouflaged financial help in the form of pocket-money for the children, holidays paid for, free meals and shopping done without re-payment. Various funds and charitable organizations may add to the widows' allowances from the National Insurance, which hardly meet subsistence needs. Pride often makes for an uneasy acceptance of National Assist- ance. In fact, the combination of financial necessity, pride, a wish for independence, and the gradual diminution of help from others, often speeds the departure of conscious sorrow. The bereaved may remark in retrospect that they have been helped to overcome their grief through the necessity to deal with practical requirements. This is reinforced by the changing attitudes of other people who begin to show they feel that the widow has now shown enough loyal sorrow, and the time has come for her to be independent and in less need of assistance.

Adjusting to the death of a loved person will always be painful and difficult; many are not helped enough. This may come about through the initial wish of the bereaved to isolate themselves. If they fail to show appreciation of well-meaning visits soon after their loss – and visitors can be very gauche – they may shrivel up the helpful intentions of their friends. Later, when they want visitors, no one may come to ease their sense of desolation, and they may be bitter over this neglect. Friends may avoid the bereaved because they do not know what to say. Some of the bereaved have remarked that they would like the clergyman to visit again after the funeral service, but he does not always come. A death, especially among elderly couples, may mean that the one who is left will, from now on, lead a life chilled by loneliness. Even if the desolation is not quite so bleak, if the relationship was very close the bereaved are likely to have lost the opportunity for the unguarded talk that they had with the one they knew so well. Widows with children feel the need to conceal their distress and watch their tongue, lest they upset the young ones. The children themselves are quite likely not to have anyone who will talk with them sincerely of their parent's death.

Society often fails to help some of the bereaved as much as it might. To improve this is not solely a matter of arranging things more efficiently. The bereaved rarely want pity and often do not want organized charity. They have a great need of personal sympathy, which comes best through the spontaneous good-will of those who know them. Clubs, societies and charitable organizations, however, are often helpful to those who are able to accept or enjoy activities of this nature. The Cruse Club, specifically designed to help widows, gives counsel and companionship to those facing the same problems, and opportunities for mutual understanding of their emotional turmoil. This organization initiated by Margaret Torrie in 1959 has been a source of strength to many.[198]

Should the medical profession institute community health projects to assist the bereaved? It has been estimated that one third to a half of immediate relatives come to doctors within a few months to obtain help over problems directly connected with their loss. The bereaved, appropriately, appear to get most assistance from relatives or close friends; but they regard doctors, as much as clergy, as their next source of help.[36] Doctors have divided views on the part they should play when bereavement is following a normal course. The medical approach is not necessarily the most suitable avenue of assistance with such human problems, although the physician and psychiatrist may have much to contribute. In Britain trained social workers will have in the future a greater degree of independence from the medical profession. It may well be that they will play an even bigger part in this field in which they already have much experience.

The church has traditionally had this function of help. Many find consolation in religious beliefs when they are bereaved. The clergy would like to do more here, particularly in helping people to regard death in a more positive way. They are severely handicapped by the fact that the majority of people in Britain do not attend church with any frequency. As long as most people in our society are unable to take advantage of the assistance that religion has to offer, the church will not be in a position to help people towards an awareness that death need not be felt solely as a fearful tragedy of loss.

Many do believe in an orthodox view of death and their faith sustains them in any uncertainty they may feel when death comes near, be it their own or of someone dear to them. Those who are not upheld by religious convictions need not resort to total mental evasion of the topic and so risk being overwhelmed when death comes too close. The majority of people face dying or the loss of a loved one with courage, even if they do not pretend to understand death. When Socrates was on trial for his life, his words were:

No one knows with regard to death whether it is not really the greatest blessing that can happen to man; but people dread it as though they were certain that it is the greatest evil. . . .[188]

When he left the court, condemned to death, he could say with calm sincerity,

Now it is time that we were going, I to die and you to live; but which of us has the happier prospect is unknown to anyone but God.

References

1. ABRAHAM, K. (1924). 'A short study of the development of the libido', *Selected Papers on Psychoanalysis*, Hogarth Press, London, 1954.
2. AITKEN-SWAN, J., 'Nursing the late cancer patient at home', *Practitioner*, 1959, *183*, p. 64.
3. AITKEN-SWAN, J., and EASSON, E.C., 'Reactions of cancer patients on being told their diagnosis', *British Medical Journal*, 1959, *1*, p. 779.
4. ALDRICH, C. K., 'The dying patient's grief', *Journal of the American Medical Association*, 1963, *184*, p. 329.
5. ALVAREZ, W. C., 'Care of the dying', *Journal of the American Medical Association*, 1952, *150*, p. 86.
6. ANDERSON, C., 'Aspects of pathological grief and mourning,' *International Journal of Psycho-Analysis*, 1949, *30*, p. 48.
7. ANSELM (1035–1109), quoted in *Approaches to Ethics*, Ed. Jones, W. T., Sontag, C., Beckner, O., and Fogelin, R. J., McGraw-Hill, New York, 1962.
8. ANTHONY, S., *The Child's Discovery of Death*, Kegan Paul, Trench & Trubner, London, 1940.
9. ASHER, R., 'Management of advanced cancer', *Proceedings of the Royal Society of Medicine*, 1955, *48*, p. 373.
10. AUTTON, N., *Death and Bereavement*, Society for Promoting Christian Knowledge, London, 1965.
11. BAILEY, M., 'A survey of the social needs of patients with incurable lung cancer', *Almoner*, 1959, *11*, p. 379.
12. BALTZELL, W. H., 'The dying patient: when the focus must be changed', *Archives of Internal Medicine*, 1971, *127*, p. 106.
13. BEALS, R. L., and HOIJER, H., *An Introduction to Anthropology*, Macmillan, New York, 1959.

14. BEAN, W. B., 'On death', *Archives of Internal Medicine*, 1958, *101*, p. 199.

15. BECKER, J. H., 'The sorrow of bereavement', *Journal of Abnormal and Social Psychology*, 1932, *27*, p. 391.

16. BEECHER, H. K., 'Relationship of significance of wounds to pain experienced', *Journal of the American Medical Association*, 1956, *161*, p. 1609.

17. BEECHER, H. K., 'The measurement of pain', *Pharmacological Reviews*, 1957, *9*, p. 59.

18. BOND, M. R. and PILOWSKY, I., 'Subjective assessment of pain and its relationship to the administration of analgesics in patients with advanced cancer', *Journal of Psychosomatic Research*, 1966, *10*, p. 203.

19. BOSWELL, J. (1791), *The Life of Samuel Johnson, LL.D.*, J. M. Dent & Sons, London, 1949.

20. BOWLBY, J., 'Grief and mourning in infancy and early childhood', *Psychoanalytic Study of the Child*, 1960, *15*, p. 9.

21. BRAIN, W. R., Opening address, *The Assessment of Pain in Man and Animals*, Ed. Keele, C.A., and Smith, R., U.F.A.W., distributors Livingstone, Edinburgh, 1962.

22. BRIM, O. G., FREEMAN, H. E., LEVINE, S. and SCOTCH, N. A., *The Dying Patient*, Russell Sage Foundation, New York, 1970.

23. *British Medical Journal*, 1968, *2*, p. 318, 'E.E.G. signs of death'.

24. BROMBERG, W., and SCHILDER, P., 'The attitude of psycho-neurotics towards death', *Psychoanalytic Review*, 1936, *23*, p. 1.

25. BROWN, F., 'Depression and childhood bereavement', *Journal of Mental Science*, 1961, *107*, p. 754.

26. BROWN, N. K., BULGER, R. J., LAWS, E. H. and THOMPSON, D. J., 'The preservation of life', *Journal of the American Medical Association*, 1970, *211*, p. 76.

27. BURNEY, F. (1784), *The Diary of Fanny Burney*, Ed. Lloyd, C., Ingram, London, 1948.

28. BURTON, L., 'Cancer children', *New Society*, 1971, p. 1040.

29. CAIN, A. C., FAST, I., and ERICKSON, M. E., 'Children's disturbed reactions to the death of a sibling', *American Journal of Orthopsychiatry*, 1964, *34*, p. 741.

30. CAMERON, G. R., 'Some remarks on the pathological process of ageing', *Ciba Foundation Colloquia on Ageing*, Ed. Wolstenholme, G. E. W., and Cameron, M. P., Vol. 1, Churchill, London, 1955.

31. CANNON, W. B., ' "Voodoo" death', *Psychosomatic Medicine*, 1957, *19*, p. 182.

32. CAPPON, D., 'The dying', *Psychiatric Quarterly*, 1959, *33*, p. 466.

33. CAPRIO, F. S., 'Ethnological attitudes toward death', *Journal of Clinical Psychopathology*, 1946, *7*, p. 737.

34. CAPRIO, F. S., 'A study of some psychological reactions during prepubescence to the idea of death', *Psychiatric Quarterly*, 1950, *24*, p. 495.

35. CARR-SAUNDERS, A. M., JONES, D. C., and MOSER, C. A., *A Survey of Social Conditions in England and Wales*, Clarendon Press, Oxford, 1958.

36. CARTWRIGHT, A. and ANDERSON, J. L., *Life before Death*. To be published 1973.

37. CHADWICK, E. (1843), *The Practice of Interment in Towns*, Clowes & Sons, London, quoted by Polson, C. J. *et al.*, 1962.

38. CHANDLER, K. A., 'Three processes of dying and their behavioural effects', *Journal of Consulting Psychology*, 1965, *29*, p. 296.

39. CHURCH ASSEMBLY BOARD FOR SOCIAL RESPONSIBILITY, *Decisions about Life and Death*, Church Information Office, London, 1965.

40. CLAYTON, P., DESMARAIS, L. and WINOKUR, G., 'A study of normal bereavement', *American Journal of Psychiatry*, 1968, *125*, p. 168.

41. COMFORT, A., *Ageing: The Biology of Senescence*, Routledge & Kegan Paul, London, 1964.

42. COX, P. R., and FORD, J. R., 'The mortality of widows shortly after widowhood', *Lancet*, 1964, *1*, p. 163.

43. CRAMOND, W. A., 'Psychotherapy of the dying patient', *British Medical Journal*, 1970, *3*, p. 389

44. DOBSON, M., TATTERSFIELD, A. E., ADLER, M. W. and MCNICOL, M. W., 'Attitudes and long-term adjustment of patients surviving cardiac arrest', *British Medical Journal*, 1971, *3*, p. 207.

45. DURKHEIM, E. (1897), *Suicide*, trans., Free Press of Glencoe, Illinois, 1951.

46. EDWARDS, I. E. S., *The Pyramids of Egypt*, Penguin Books, Harmondsworth, 1961.

47. EISSLER, K. R., *The Psychiatrist and the Dying Patient*, International Universities Press, New York, 1955.

48. ENGEL, G. L., 'Is grief a disease?', *Psychosomatic Medicine*, 1961, *23*, p. 18.

49. EPICURUS (342–270 B.C.), Letter to Menoeceus quoted in *Approaches to Ethics*, Ed. Jones, W. T., Sontag, C., Beckner, M.O. and Fogelin, R. J., McGraw-Hill, New York, 1962.

50. EUTHANASIA SOCIETY, *A Plan for Voluntary Euthanasia*, London, 1962.

51. EXTON-SMITH, A. N., 'Terminal illness in the aged', *Lancet*, 1961, *2*, p. 305.

52. FEIFEL, H., 'Attitudes of mentally ill patients toward death', *Journal of Nervous and Mental Diseases*, 1955, *122*, p. 375.

53. FEIFEL, H., 'Older persons look at death', *Geriatrics*, 1956, *11*, p. 127.

54. FEIFEL, H., 'Attitudes toward death in some normal and mentally ill populations', *The Meaning of Death*, Ed. Feifel, H., McGraw-Hill, New York, 1959.

55. FEINSTEIN, H. M., PAUL, N., and ESMIOL, P., 'Group therapy for mothers with infanticidal impulses', *American Journal of Psychiatry*, 1964, *120*, p. 882.

56. FREUD, S. (1915), 'Our attitude towards death', *Collected Papers*, Hogarth Press, London, 1925.

57. FREUD, S. (1917), 'Mourning and melancholia', *Collected Papers*, Hogarth Press, London, 1925.

58. FREUD, S., *Beyond the Pleasure Principle* (1920), *The Complete Psychological Works of Sigmund Freud*, Hogarth Press, London, 1951.

59. FREUD, S., *The Libido Theory* (1923), *The Complete Psychological Works of Sigmund Freud*, Hogarth Press, London, 1951.

60. GAULT, D., *A Journey*, Chatto and Windus, London, 1968.

61. GAVEY, C. J., *The Management of the Hopeless Case*, Lewis, London, 1952.

62. GAVEY, C. J., 'Discussion on palliation in cancer', *Proceedings of the Royal Society of Medicine*, 1955, *48*, p. 703.

63. GERLE, B., LUNDÉN, G., and SANDBLOM, P., 'The patient with in-operable cancer from the psychiatric and social standpoints', *Cancer*, 1960, *13*, p. 1206.

64. GILBERTSEN, V. A., and WANGENSTEEN, O. H., 'Should the doctor tell the patient that the disease is cancer?', in *The Physician and the Total Care of the Cancer Patient*, American Cancer Society, New York, 1961.

65. GLASER, B. G., and STRAUSS, A. L., *Awareness of Dying*, Aldine, Chicago, 1965.

66. GLASER, B. G. and STRAUSS, A. L., *Time for Dying*, Aldine, Chicago, 1968.

67. GOLDMAN, I., 'The Kwaikiutl Indians of Vancouver Island', in

Co-operation and Competition Among Primitive People, Ed. Mead, M., McGraw-Hill, New York, 1937.

68. GOTTLIEB, C., 'Modern art and death', *The Meaning of Death*, Ed. Feifel, H., McGraw-Hill, New York, 1959.

69. GORER, G., *Exploring English Character*, Cresset Press, London 1955.

70. GORER, G., *Death, Grief and Mourning*, Cresset Press, London, 1965.

71. GREER, S., 'The relationship between parental loss and attempted suicide', *British Journal of Psychiatry*, 1964, *110*, p. 698

72. HARRIS, E. G., 'Physician, clergyman and patient in terminal illness', *Pennsylvania Medical Journal*, 1951, *54*, p. 541.

73. HAWKES, J., *A Guide to Prehistoric and Roman Antiquities of England and Wales*, Chatto & Windus, London, 1952.

74. HEAD, H., *Studies in Neurology*, Vol. 2, Frowde, Hodder and Stoughton, London, 1920.

75. HEIM, A., 'Über den Tod durch Absturz', *Jb. Schweiz. Alpenclub*, quoted in *General Psychopathology*, Jaspers, K., trans., University Press, Manchester, 1963.

76 HENDERSON, J. G., WITTKOWER, E. D., and LOUGHEED, M. N., 'A psychiatric investigation of the delay factor in patient-to-doctor presentation in cancer', *Journal of Psychosomatic Research*, 1958, *3*, p. 27.

77. HERBERT, C. C., 'Psychophysiology of death', *Physiology of Emotions*, Ed. Simon, A., Herbert, C. C., and Straus, R., C. C. Thomas, Springfield, Illinois, 1961.

78. HERTZ, R. (1909), *Death and The Right Hand*, Trans. Needham, R. and C., University Press, Aberdeen, 1960.

79. HILGARD, J. R., and NEWMAN, M. F., 'Anniversaries in mental illness', *Psychiatry*, 1959, *22*, p. 113.

80. HINTON, J. M., 'The physical and mental distress of the dying', *Quarterly Journal of Medicine*, 1963, *32*, p. 1.

81. HINTON, J. M., 'Distress in the dying', *Medicine in Old Age*, Ed. Agate, J. N., Pitman, London, 1965.

82. HINTON, J. M., 'Facing death', *Journal of Psychosomatic Research*, 1966, *10*, p. 22.

83. HINTON, J. M., 'Assessing the views of the dying', *Social Science and Medicine*, 1971, *5*, p. 37.

84. HINTON, J. M., 'Psychiatric Consultation in patients with fatal illness', *Proceedings of the Royal Society of Medicine*, 1972.

85. HORDER, T. J., 'Signs and symptoms of impending death', *Practitioner*, 1948, *161*, p. 13.

86. *Hospital Medicine*, 1967, I, p. 563, 'Telling the relatives'.

87. HUGHES, H. L. G., *Peace at the Last*, Calouste Gulbenkian Foundation, London, 1960.

88. INOGUCHI, R. T., NAKAJIMA, T., and PINEAU, R., *The Divine Wind: Japan's Kamikaze Force in World War II*, Hutchinson, London, 1959.

89. INSTITUTE OF MEDICINE OF CHICAGO, *Terminal Care for Cancer Patients*, Chicago, 1950.

90. ISAACS, B., 'Geriatric patients: do their families care?' *British Medical Journal*, 1971, *4*, p. 282.

91. ISAACS, B., GUNN, J., MCKECHAN, A., MCMILLAN, I. and NEVILLE, Y., 'The concept of pre-death', *Lancet*, 1971, *1*, p. 1115.

92. JACKSON, E. N., 'Grief and religion', *The Meaning of Death*, Ed. Feifel, H., McGraw-Hill, New York, 1960.

93. JACOBS, P. A., COURT BROWN, W. M., and DOLL, R., 'Distribution of human chromosome counts in relation to age', *Nature*, London, 1961, *191*, p. 1178.

94. JOINT NATIONAL CANCER SURVEY COMMITTEE, *Report on a National Survey Concerning Patients with Cancer Nursed at Home*, Marie Curie Memorial, London, 1952.

95. JARVINEN, K. A. J., 'Can ward rounds be a danger to patients with myocardial infarction?', *British Medical Journal*, 1955, *1*, p. 318.

96. JONES, K., 'Suicide and the hospital service', *British Journal of Psychiatry*, 1965, *111*, p. 625.

97. JUNG, C. G., 'The soul and death' (1934), *The Collected Works of C. G. Jung*, Routledge & Kegan Paul, London.

98. JUNG, C. G., 'Psychological commentary on "The Tibetan Book of the Dead" ' (1935), *The Collected Works of C. G. Jung*, Routledge & Kegan Paul, London.

99. KALISH, R. A., 'Social distance and the dying', *Community Mental Health Journal*, 1966, *2*, p. 152.

100. KEELE, C. A., and SMITH, R., *The Assessment of Pain in Man and Animals*, U.F.A.W., distributors Livingstone, Edinburgh, 1962.

101. KELLY, W. D., and FRIESEN, S. R., 'Do cancer patients want to be told?', *Surgery*, 1950, *27*, p. 822.

102. KLEIN, M., 'Mourning and its relation to manic-depressive states', (1940), *Contributions to Psychoanalysis, 1921–1945*, Hogarth Press, London, 1948.

103. KLINE, N. S., and SOBIN, J., 'The psychological management of

cancer cases', *Journal of the American Medical Association*, 1951, *146*, p. 1547.

104. KNUDSON, A. G., and NATTERSON, J. M., 'Practice of pediatrics – participation of parents in the hospital care of fatally ill children', *Pediatrics*, 1960, *26*, p. 482.

105. KRAUS, A. S., and LILIENFELD, A. M., 'Some epidemiological aspects of the high mortality rate in the young widowed group', *Journal of Chronic Diseases*, 1959, *10*, p. 207.

106. KÜBLER-ROSS, E., *On Death and Dying*, Tavistock Publications, London, 1970.

107. LACK, D. (1943), *The Life of the Robin*, Penguin Books, Harmondsworth, 1953.

108. LACK, D., *The Natural Regulation of Animal Numbers*, Oxford University Press, London, 1954.

109. LAFORET, E. G., 'The "hopeless" case', *Archives of Internal Medicine*, 1963, *112*, p. 314.

110. *Lancet*, 1961, *2*, p. 351, 'Euthanasia'.

111. *Lancet*, 1964, *1*, p. 1201, 'Not so great expectations'.

112. *Lancet*, 1965, *2*, p. 858, 'Help for the invalid's family'.

113. LASAGNA, L., 'Physicians' behaviour toward the dying patient', in *The Dying Patient*, ed. Brim, O. G., Freeman, H. E., Levine, S. and Scotch, N. A., Russell Sage Foundation, New York, 1970.

114. LEAK, W. N., 'The care of the dying', *Practitioner*, 1948, *161*, p. 80.

115. LE GROS CLARK, W. E., *History of the Primates*, British Museum, London, 1962.

116. LEHRMAN, S. R., 'Reactions to untimely death', *Psychiatric Quarterley*, 1956, *30*, p. 564.

117. LERNER, M., 'When, why and where people die', in *The Dying Patient*, ed. Brim, O. G., Freeman, H. E., Levine, S. and Scotch, N. A., Russell Sage Foundation, New York, 1970.

118. LESTER, D., 'Attitudes toward death today and thirty-five years ago', *Omega*, 1971, *2*, p. 168.

119. LEWIS, A. J., 'Melancholia: A clinical survey of depressive states', *Journal of Mental Science*, 1934, *80*, p. 277.

120. LINDEMANN, E., 'Symptomatology and management of acute grief', *American Journal of Psychiatry*, 1944, *101*, p. 141.

121. LINDEMANN, E., 'Modifications in the course of ulcerative colitis in relationship to changes in life situations and reaction patterns', *Proceedings of the Association for Research in Nervous and Mental Disease*, 1950, *29*, p. 706.

122. LOWE, C. R., 'Care of the chronic sick (investigation of 393 patients seeking admission to a hospital for the chronic sick)', *British Medical Journal*, 1950, *2*, p. 699.

123. LOWTHER, C. P. and WILLIAMSON, J., 'Old people and their relatives', *Lancet*, 1966, *2*, p. 1459.

124. MADDISON, D. and VIOLA, A., 'The health of widows in the year following bereavement', *Journal of Psychosomatic Research*, 1968, *12*, p. 297.

125. MADDISON, D. and WALKER, W. L., 'Factors affecting the outcome of conjugal bereavement', *British Journal of Psychiatry*, 1967, *113*, p. 1057.

126. MALINOWSKY, B., *Myth in Primitive Psychology*, Kegan Paul, Trench & Trubner, London, 1926.

127. MARRIS, P., *Widows and Their Families*, Routledge & Kegan Paul, London, 1958.

128. MEAD, M., *Sex and Temperament in Three Primitive Societies*, Routledge, London, 1935.

129. MEDAWAR, P. B., 'The definition and measurement of senescence', in *Ciba Foundation Colloquia on Ageing*, Eds. Wolstenholme, G. E. W., and Cameron, M. P., Churchill, London, 1955.

130. MCCULLOCH, M., *Peoples of Sierra Leone Protectorate*, International African Institute, London, 1950.

131. MCDERMOTT, N. and COBB, S., 'Psychogenic factors in asthma', *Psychosomatic Medicine*, 1939, *1*, p. 204.

132. MCCAY, C. M., POPE, F., and LUNSFORD, W., 'Experimental prolongation of the life span', *Bulletin of the New York Academy of Medicine*, 1956, *32*, p. 91.

133. MIDDLETON, W. C., 'Some reactions towards death among college students', *Journal of Abnormal and Social Psychology*, 1936, *31*, p. 2.

134. MITFORD, J., *The American Way of Death*, Hutchinson, London, 1963.

135. MONTAIGNE (1573), *Essays of Michel de Montaigne*, trans., Ed. Hazlitt, W. C., Bell, London, 1892.

136. MORTON-WILLIAMS, P., 'Yoruba responses to the fear of death', *Africa*, 1960, *30*, p. 34.

137. MURPHY, G., 'Discussion', *The Meaning of Death*, Ed. Feifel, H., McGraw-Hill, New York, 1959.

138. NAGY, M. H., 'The child's theories concerning death', *Journal of Genetic Psychology*, 1948, *73*, p. 3.

139. NARDINI, J. E., 'Survival factors in American prisoners of war of the Japanese', *American Journal of Psychiatry*, 1952, *109*, p. 241.

140. NATTERSON, J. M., and KNUDSON, A. G., 'Observations concerning fear of death in fatally ill children and their mothers', *Psychosomatic Medicine*, 1960, *22*, p. 456.

141. NORTON, J., 'Treatment of a dying patient', *Psychoanalytic Study of the Child*, 1963, *18*, p. 541.

142. OGILVIE, H., 'Journey's end', *Practitioner*, 1957, *179*, p. 584.

143. OKEN, D., 'What to tell cancer patients', *Journal of the American Medical Association*, 1961, *175*, p. 1120.

144. ORBACH, C. E., 'The multiple meanings of the loss of a child', *American Journal of Psychotherapy*, 1959, *13*, p. 906.

145. ORLANS, H., 'Some attitudes towards death', *Diogenes*, 1957, *19*, p. 73.

146. OSLER, W., *Science and Immortality*, Constable, London, 1906.

147. PARKES, C. M., *Reactions to Bereavement*, M.D. Thesis, London University, 1962.

148. PARKES, C. M., 'Grief as an illness', *New Society*, 1964, *3*, p. 11.

149. PARKES, C. M., 'Recent bereavement as a cause of mental illness', *British Journal of Psychiatry*, 1964, *110*, p. 198.

150. PARKES, C. M., 'Effects of bereavement on physical and mental health – a study of the medical records of widows', *British Medical Journal*, 1964, *2*, p. 274.

151. PARKES, C. M., 'Bereavement and mental illness', *British Journal of Medical Psychology*, 1965, *38*, p. 1.

152. PARKES, C. M., 'The first year of bereavement', *Psychiatry*, 1970, *33*, p. 444.

153. PARKES, C. M., BENJAMIN, B. and FITZGERALD, R. G., 'Broken heart: a statistical study of increased mortality among widowers', *British Medical Journal*, 1969, *1*, p. 740.

154. PENNYBACKER, J., 'Management of intractable pain', *Proceedings of the Royal Society of Medicine*, 1963, *56*, p. 191.

155. PIUS XII, 'Concerning re-animation', address to the *International Congress of Anaesthetists*, Rome, 24 November 1957, quoted by Collins, V. J., 'Fatalities in Anaesthesia and Surgery', *Journal of the American Medical Association*, 1960, *172*, p. 549.

156. PLATT, R., 'Reflections on ageing and death', *Lancet*, 1963, *1*, p. 1.

157. PLATT, B., 'Euthanasia', *Proceedings of the Royal Society of Medicine*, 1970, *63*, p. 659.

158. POLSON, C. J., BRITTAIN, R. P., and MARSHALL, T. K., *The Disposal of the Dead*, English Universities Press, London, 1962.

159. RICHTER, C. P., 'On the phenomenon of sudden death in animals and man', *Psychosomatic Medicine*, 1957, *19*, p. 191.

160. REES, W. D., 'The hallucinations of widowhood', *British Medical Journal*, 1971, *4*, p. 37.

161. REES, W. D., and LUTKINS, S. G., 'Mortality of bereavement', *British Medical Journal*, 1967, *4*, p. 13.

162. REGISTRAR-GENERAL, *Statistical Review of England and Wales for the year 1969*, Part I, H.M. Stationery Office, London, 1971.

163. REGISTRAR-GENERAL, Occupational Mortality Tables, *Decennial Supplement, England and Wales, 1961*, H.M. Stationery Office, London, 1971.

164. RILEY, J. W., 'What people think about death', in *The Dying Patient*, ed. Brim, O. G., Freeman, H. E., Levine, S. and Scotch, N. A., Russell Sage Foundation, New York, 1970.

165. ROSENTHAL, H. R., 'Psychotherapy for the dying', *American Journal of Psychotherapy*, 1957, *11*, p. 626.

166. ROSSMAN, I., and KISSICK, W. L., 'Home care and the cancer patient', *The Physician and the Total Care of the Cancer Patient*, American Cancer Society, New York, 1961.

167. ROTH, M., 'The phobic-anxiety depersonalization syndrome' *Proceedings of the Rotal Society of Medicine*, 1959, *52*, p. 587.

168. RUSSELL, BERTRAND, *A History of Western Philosophy*, Allen & Unwin, London, 1946.

169. RUSSELL, J. K., and MILLER, M. R., 'Care of women with terminal pelvic cancer', *British Medical Journal*, 1964, *1*, p. 1214.

170. RYLE, J. A., *Fears May Be Liars*, Allen & Unwin, London, 1941.

171. SAINSBURY, P. *Suicide in London*, Chapman & Hall, London, 1955.

172. SANDARS, N. K., *The Epic of Gilgamesh*, Penguin Books, Harmondsworth, 1960.

173. SAUNDERS, C., *Care of the Dying*, Macmillan, London, 1959.

174. SAUNDERS, C., 'Euthanasia', *Lancet*, 1961, *2*, p. 548.

175. SAUNDERS, C., 'The treatment of intractable pain in terminal cancer', *Proceedings of the Royal Society of Medicine*, 1963, *56*, p. 195.

176. SAUNDERS, C., 'The management of terminal illness', *Hospital Medicine*, 1966–7, pp. 225, 317, 433.

177. SCHLESINGER, B. and MACRAE, A., 'The widow and widower and remarriage', *Omega*, *2*, p. 10.

178. SEAGER, C. P., and FLOOD, R. A., 'Suicide in Bristol', *British Journal of Psychiatry*, 1965, *111*, p. 919.

179. SHELDON, J. H., *The Social Medicine of Old Age*, Oxford University Press, London, 1948.

180. SHELDON, J. H., *Report to the Birmingham Regional Hospital Board on its Geriatric Services*, Birmingham Regional Hospital Board, 1961.

181. SHELELIG, H., and FALK, H. (1937), 'Royal ship-burials in Viking times', *The World of the Past*, Ed. Hawkes, J., Thames & Hudson, London, 1963.

182. SIMMONS, L. W., *The Role of the Aged in Primitive Society*, Yale University Press, New Haven, 1945.

183. SKEET, M., *Home from Hospital*, Florence Nightingale Memorial Committee, 1970.

184. SLATER, E., 'The biologist and the fear of death', *The Plain View*, 1958, *12*, p. 29.

185. SLATER, E., 'Health service or sickness service?', *British Medical Journal*, 1971, *4*, p. 734.

186. SMART, N., 'Death in the Judaeo-Christian tradition', in *Man's Concern with Death*, Toynbee, A. *et al.*, Hodder and Stoughton, London, 1968.

187. SMART, N., 'Some inadequacies of recent Christian thought about death', in *Man's Concern with Death*, Toynbee, A. *et. al.*, Hodder and Stoughton, London, 1968.

188. SOCRATES (399 B.C.), from 'The Apology', *The Last Days of Socrates*, Plato, trans. Tredennick, H., Penguin Books, Harmondsworth, 1954.

189. STEKEL, W., *Compulsion and Doubt*, Peter Nevill, London, 1950.

190. STENGEL, E., *Suicide and Attempted Suicide*, Penguin Books, Harmondsworth, 1964.

191. STERN, K. WILLIAMS, G. M., and PRADOS, M., 'Grief reactions in later life', *American Journal of Psychiatry*, 1951, *108*, p. 289.

192. STEWART, I., 'Suicide: The influence of organic disease', *Lancet*, 1960, *2*, p. 919.

193. SWENSON, W. M., 'Attitudes toward death among the aged', *Minnesota Medicine*, 1959, *42*, p. 399.

194. TAS, J., 'Psychical disorders among inmates of concentration camps and repatriates', *Psychiatric Quarterly*, 1951, *25*, p. 679.

195. TAYLOR, G. R., *The Angel Makers*, Heinemann, London, 1958.

196. THOMSON, A. P., 'Discussion on the problems of old age', *Proceedings of the Royal Society of Medicine*, 1950, *43*, p. 929.

197. THOMSON, A. P., LOWE, C. R., and MCKEOWN, T., *The Care of the Ageing and Chronic Sick*, Livingstone, Edinburgh, 1951.

198. TORRIE, M., *Begin Again*, Dent, London, 1970.

199. TOWNSEND, P., *The Family Life of Old People*, Routledge & Kegan

References 209

Paul, London, 1957, and Penguin Books, Harmondsworth, 1963.

200. TOWNSEND, P., *The Development of Home and Welfare Services for Old People 1946–60*, Association of Directors of Welfare Services, Leicester, 1961.

201. TOWNSEND, P., *The Last Refuge*, Routledge & Kegan Paul, London, 1962.

202. TOYNBEE, A., 'Traditional attitudes towards death', in *Man's Concern with Death*, Toynbee, A. *et al.*, Hodder and Stoughton, London, 1968.

203. TURNER, G. (1884), *Samoa. A Hundred Years Ago and Long Before*, quoted in *The Role of the Aged in Primitive Society*, Simmons, L. W., Yale University Press, New Haven, 1945.

204. VOLKART, E. H., 'Bereavement and mental health', *Explorations in Social Psychiatry*, Ed. Leighton, A. H., Clausen, J. A., and Wilson, R. N., Basic Books, New York, 1957.

205. WAHL, C. W., 'The fear of death', *Bulletin of the Menninger Clinic*, 1958, *22*, p. 214.

206. WAUGH, E., *The Loved One*, Chapman & Hall, London, 1948.

207. WEBER, F. P. *Aspects of Death and Correlated Aspects of Life in Art, Epigram and Poetry*, Unwin, London, 1918.

208. WEISMAN, A. D., and HACKETT, T. P., 'Predilection to death', *Psychosomatic Medicine*, 1961, *23*, p. 232.

209. *Which*, Consumer Association, London, February 1961, 'Funerals'.

210. WILKES, E., 'Cancer outside hospital', *Lancet*, 1964, *1*, p. 1379.

211. WILKES, E., 'Terminal cancer at home', *Lancet*, 1965, *1*, p. 799.

212. WILLIAMS, G., 'Euthanasia', *Proceedings of the Royal Society of Medicine*, 1971, *63*, p. 663.

213. WOOLLEY, C. L. (1929), *Ur of the Chaldees*, Penguin Books, Harmondsworth, 1938.

214. WORCESTER, A., *The Care of the Aged, the Dying and the Dead*, C. C. Thomas, Springfield, Illinois, 1935.

215. WRETMARK, G., 'A study in grief reactions', *Acta psychiatrica et neurologica Scandinavica Suppl.*, 1959, *136*, p. 292.

216. YOUNG, M., and WILLMOTT, P., *Family and Kinship in East London*, Routledge & Kegan Paul, London, 1957, and Penguin Books, Harmondsworth, 1962.

217. YOUNG, M., BENJAMIN, B., and WALLIS, C., 'The mortality of widowers', *Lancet*, 1963, *2*, p. 454.

218. YUDKIN, S., 'Children and death', *Lancet*, 1967, *1*, p. 37.

219. ZILBOORG, G., 'Fear of death', *Psychoanalytic Quarterly*, 1943, *12*, p. 465.

Index

More about Penguins and Pelicans

Children Under Stress

Sula Wolff

'This is an admirable book, which deserves to
be widely read, not only by those who are
professionally concerned with disturbed and
unhappy children, but by that very large number
of parents who are worried from time to time
about their children's behaviour and who are
uncertain about when to seek expert advice ... It is
the best summary known to me of what can be
achieved by child psychiatry, and an excellent
account of the causes and common manifestations
of emotional disturbance in children' – Dr
Anthony Storr

The Psychology of Human Ageing

D. B. Bromley

Second Edition

The Study of adult life and old age is becoming
increasingly important, but has long been a
neglected area of knowledge. Dr Bromley, who is
both a psychologist and a gerontologist, here
provides a general introduction to the subject.

The author has enlarged, extensively revised and
updated this second edition of a widely used
book. He deals with a wide range of social,
psychological and behavioural aspects of human
ageing – including middle age and the terminal
stage – and shows how they are related to
biological ageing. He traces the history of man's
concern with ageing and examines some of the
technical problems encountered in research.

Dr Bromley's book, which the *Sociological
Review* called 'a welcome and valuable
introduction to the psychology of human
ageing', will be valuable both to the general
and to the professional reader.